D0337520

CYNTHIA HEIMEL

ADVANCED SEX TIPS FOR GIRLS

This Time It's Personal

A FIRESIDE BOOK

PUBLISHED BY SIMON & SCHUSTER

New York London Toronto Sydney Singapore

Fireside
Rockefeller Center
1230 Avenue of the Americas
New York, NY 10020

First Fireside Edition 2003

FIRESIDE and colophon are registered trademarks
of Simon & Schuster, Inc.

For information about special discounts for bulk purchases,
please contact Simon & Schuster Special Sales:
1-800-456-6798 or business@simonandschuster.com.

Book design by Ellen R. Sasahara

Manufactured in the United States of America

1 3 5 7 9 10 8 6 4 2

The Library of Congress has cataloged the Simon & Schuster edition as
follows:
Heimel, Cynthia, date.
Advanced sex tips for girls : this time it's personal / Cynthia Heimel.
p. cm.
1. Sex—Humor. I. Title.
PN6231.S34 H439 2002
818'.5402—dc21 2001057564

ISBN 0-684-84922-4
0-684-85645-X (Pbk)

To Michael Longacre and Dalling

CONTENTS

CONTENTS

I

PROLOGUE TO A NERVOUS BREAKDOWN

1

GIDDY!

IT WAS JUNE 1996. I REMEMBER IT AS IF IT WERE yesterday. Sometimes I feel as if it *were* yesterday.

I was sitting on the bed at the Paramount Hotel in Manhattan on the night he asked me to marry him. Complicated and addled New York woman, sitting in a complicated, addled New York hotel, ice available whenever needed or appropriate, is as usual talking on the phone, *Vogue* on lap, when his words etched the air.

"Will you marry me?" Woodrow asked.

"Yes," I answered without hesitation.

There had been clues. The five-hour phone conversations. The crucial and palpable need to call him during a family wedding to say, "You're not going to believe this, but there are rich people in Scottsdale who don't like Jews." The odd coincidences that we won't go into. The way my insides would puddle when I read anything he wrote.

It took us so long to meet. I had been looking at my watch, humming and tapping my foot for an entire decade. There were two Mr. Wrongs in quick succession. I had given up. We corresponded before we met. One of those Internet billboard systems. I knew he was the right one but I didn't want to meet him because he would be the wrong one. We would look at each other and say, "And who are you?" All that writing, all that talking, and we would look at each other and say, "Heh-heh, gotta go, left the iron on, let's have lunch maybe never." But I finally said I would meet him at a bookstore in Long Beach, and I pulled into the parking lot and there he was. One look and I was fucking dead. I was dead fucked. I knew it and I didn't care.

And it was hours, agonizing hours later when he spilled two quarts of iced coffee on me and I knew, I just knew, he wanted to grab me by the hair. And pull.

By the end of the evening we were finishing each other's sentences. By the end of a week we were on a runaway train slamming blindly through stations at a hundred miles an hour. The passengers waiting on the platform for the train, arms akimbo, mouths agape, started yelling, "Wait! Stop! Are you crazy?" In New York the train sped up. I said yes to him without hesitation.

S. said, "I don't want you to have a boyfriend. I want you to be always available to me."

L. said, "Oh please, you're being just so ridiculous. You don't know what you're doing."

B. said, "I am so jealous, what about me? Will I be the last one alone?"

K. said, "Fuck you, fuck you, fuck you!"

I watched their mouths move as I sped past them.

I flew home to LA. At the airport he was waiting with a dozen red roses and a blue box from Tiffany. He led me to a chair. I stumbled and stared into my lap. I opened the box and found an engagement ring. He got down on his knees.

"Will you marry me?" he asked again.

"Yes," I answered, and he slipped the ring on my finger.

Later he said, "I want to get married very, very, very soon."

"Wait at least six months," said my shrink.

"Okay," I said.

"No, wait at least a year," said my son.

"Okay," I said.

Several days later at 2:00 A.M. the love of my life and I got into the car with a thermos of coffee, a loaf of sourdough bread, and a small dog and headed east on Interstate 15 toward Las Vegas.

Sally sat on my lap, 9.8 pounds of doggie love concentrate. My future groom drove.

We passed through interminable LA suburbs and hit the stone strange Mojave. We drove all night, ignoring the stars while I looked for the glint of coyote eyes.

What would my son think? How would I tell my shrink? My bladder began to chatter. I asked my intended to pull over by an abandoned gas station and got out and peed on a flat rock. Clouds of steam and dust rose up. A big black dog drowsed a few yards away but I did not say hello.

At the Clark County Court House people were checking their guns as they went through the metal detectors. We filled out marriage applications in pencil. I gave myself a new middle initial, what the hell. We didn't have to show driver's licenses or anything. At all.

The block walk to the marriage commissioner was a Bataan Death March Jr. It was 107 degrees. Sally trotted hazily.

The marriage commissioner was a fat man who was enveloped in a cloud of Aqua Velva. His toupee was as big as the Ritz. "Wait right here," he said to us, and went to round up a witness.

Sally and I left the office and went to the ladies' room. I wanted to wash my face, have a drink. I wanted to think.

I stood in the ladies' room with the faucet running, splashing my face while Sally danced around my ankles. I thought of the Mudd Club. I thought of doing so many drugs one night that a friend wanted to drink my urine. I thought of the smell of Lester's coat the last time I hugged him. I thought of Saban and Musto and Peacock and the Odeon and a specific anxiety attack I call the blancmange. I thought of exactly where you can get a cab in Chelsea at 5:30 P.M. I don't know what my betrothed was thinking.

I plucked white dog hair off my black linen shirt as I lost myself in memories of sitting in countless coffee shops on countless Manhattan corners drinking endless cups of coffee with girlfriends endlessly discussing men and how fucked up they were and what did it mean when they said, "I'll call you Thursday." And how we reassured each other stoutly that of course it was the men, of course there was nothing wrong with us, but inside the voice of sabotage was keening, "You are so fat and you are stupid and you're not supposed to smell like that and who are you kidding with that hair and those neurotic thoughts and that hellish neediness that desperation and that huge butt? Do you really think black lipstick is going to help?"

But we were stouthearted with each other, bolstering each other against disappointment and confusion, drinking coffee, drinking more coffee, discussing, discussing. Never realizing that there was nothing wrong with us, that it was, more often than not, the men.

And I thought, "Me, married?"

Haha.

Ha.

2

"COMPLICITY," HE SAID

I WAS IN AUSTRALIA ON A BOOK TOUR. THEY LINED UP one million interviews and I had to keep talking about myself, which is less fun than you may think.

"So, is there a man in your life?" I was asked forty-two thousand times.

And God help me, I told them all about the man in my life. I made an entire human being into shtick. "Yeah, he's a construction worker. Women are into rough trade now. It's the latest thing." I even made a game attempt to extrapolate and explain this relationship as a bona-fide sociological phenomenon:

"Because women are no longer defined by their men, no

Originally appeared in *Playboy* magazine.

longer evaluated by the company we keep, we no longer need men who make more money than we do, or men with superior social standing. We just need someone with a good heart who likes animals." At the time it seemed like a sound theory. Sure, I was flying in the face of the alleged biological imperative, but what the hell.

I got home from Australia and broke up with the construction worker and got a good half-dozen columns out of it, plus many delightful hours of girlfriend postmortem coffee talk.

Then I met another guy and immediately went to England on a book tour. Again every interviewer wanted not only the broad outlines but every single nuance of my romantic life. I trotted out my new story for radio, TV and print, a story that, trust me, by the third time you hear it would make you just as nauseous as I was.

My English girlfriends were riveted by the new romance, especially since this guy seemed to send e-mail with every third breath. This e-mail was of course read, cataloged, cross-indexed and exhaustively analyzed by the girls. Three whole dinners were spent on e-mail #7, in which the L-word reared its ugly head.

"This is so wonderful. I am living through you vicariously," said Gillian. "I don't think my pulse rate's been up this high in years. When you're married you don't get to discuss your sex life or the L-word or *anything* with your girlfriends."

(Gillian had been married for five years. Before she married Gilbert I was privy to everything. Gilbert couldn't say "Not tonight, poppet, I have a headache," without me hearing of it within fifteen minutes. If Gillian had to, she'd call me from the bathroom.)

"Well, Gillian, how is married life? Are you two happy?" I asked.

"We're perfectly fine," she said quellingly, giving me the hairy eyeball.

Fortunately for my writing life my new romantic interest turned out to be, not to put too fine a point on it, an utter creep. Oh, the columns about the fights! The incessant 2:00 A.M. conferences with friends!

"I feel like I'm piloting this ship alone," I said to Woodrow (not his real name), a pal I met on the Well, my online community. Woodrow wrote columns for the alternative press like I did. We exchanged scads of e-mail, then when my relationship with creep-boy started crashing and burning we spent hours on the phone.

"Get out now, leave everything, don't pack even an overnight case!" he would shout. He took to calling at 2:00 A.M. (PST) just to make sure I hadn't overdosed or anything and I'd tell him everything. One night I was sniffling and hiccuping from a recent sobbing frenzy.

"The thing is," he said, "good relationships should be based on complicity. Yours isn't."

Complicity? This was an entirely new concept. Sure, I'd fantasized that someday I'd find someone and it would be the two of us against the world, the dream team taking on all comers. But the only time I'd experienced such a dynamic was as a mother. My son and I constantly watch each other's backs and bring each other chicken soup.

But complicity with a lover? Nah. In my universe lovers were more like enemies. There were power struggles, infidelities, those hideous commitment conversations, the withholding of love or sex or both, plus the ever-popular "I-don't-care-about-you-as-much-as-you-care-about-me" dynamic. To me, complicity meant hanging out with my girlfriends, plotting relationship maneuvers.

Complicity, huh? That must be why married people are markedly mute. Marriage has nothing to do with these bloody sieges I called romance. Instead of emotional bungee-jumping, my married friends were apparently doing loyalty, compassion and trust. How goofy is *that*?

3

THE FIFTIES—ROOT OF ALL PANTY GIRDLES

IN THE BEGINNING, THERE WAS THE PANTY GIRDLE. THIS was a fabulously cruel instrument of torture. It was made of adamant rubber. It cut into our waists, making it hurt to breathe. But the waist pain was a day in the park compared to the thigh pain. It rolled up our thighs into bands of gangrene-inducing death. Many women became addicted to barbiturates. The only way to check the dread thigh roll-up was to wear stockings, which caused an entirely different version of pain, especially when a garter snapped and caused massive thigh hematoma.

"You'll wear it and like it, little missy!" said my mother when

I was *eleven.* My torture, and the torture of millions of little girls my age (and younger!), brought a sea change to the world.

Without panty girdles, modern feminism might never have been invented. The panty girdle was the straw that broke the back of the patriarchy. They had gone too far!

Panty girdles appeared in the fifties, a scary and dreadful decade. Well, sure, it seems very cute today with the ubiquitous McCoy flowerpots and the Eames chairs and fabulous poodle skirts. And it is true that in the fifties you could buy a George Nelson lamp for $4.98.

What kind of decade would have TV commercials featuring women wearing white gloves and sashaying around each other's houses, testing every surface for dust? Or produce movies where the entire plot pivoted on whether or not Doris Day lost her virginity to Rock Hudson before marriage?

A tiny little girl, I would watch these movies, and I would think, "Someday my Prince will come." I would lie in my bed, my dozens of stuffed animals tucked in and kissed good-night, and I would pretend that I was waiting for my husband to come join me.

During the day I would while away my free time by pretending to be acting in soap commercials. I would scrub the bathroom sink meticulously and declaim, "See how quick and easy!" to the bathroom mirror.

I blame the fifties entirely for this behavior. And I blame the forties for the fifties.

The forties made all men insane. They were in airplanes and on beaches and wherever they were people tried to kill them. The ones who didn't die watched their pals' heads blow up. Even if a guy had a cushy desk job, he had the dreadful knowledge that somewhere right then there were concentration camps, and it was up to them to save the whole fucking world. Therefore: insanity.

And insanity for the women at home too, waiting and terrified.

Then the war was over. The women had been out there in the world working, but now that would never do since men needed to feel safe, and to feel safe after watching people's entrails spill all over the ground meant being in total utter complete and categorical control. So then these irrevocably traumatized men got all the women pregnant and constructed from scratch that most hideous of all postwar monsters: the modern businessman. Every man put on one of those cool iridescent sharkskin suits except for a Dr. Benjamin Spock, who wrote a book—a book that told women not to breast-feed and to keep their babies on a strict feeding schedule. Their babies grew up to become acid heads in the sixties who named all their children Treetop or Garage.

Plus there were all those unironic crew cuts. It has been a deep dark secret of the scientific community that the unironic crew cut causes not only its wearer but also every human within one hundred yards to become a fatuous, bullying, conformity-obsessed drone.

These were the ten unironic crew-cut commandments:

1. Thou shall not be weird!
2. Thou must move to the suburbs and cultivate thy tedious lawn!
3. Thou must revere all authority figures no matter how idiotic! Or depressing!
4. When in doubt, BULLY.

5. Insure thyself against life.
6. Anything different or new is SCARY.
7. Anything scary is WRONG and EVIL.
8. Beware of queers, sluts, beatniks, foreigners, coloreds and Communists!
9. Thou may question nothing!
10. If thy weirdness offends you, shoot thyself!

It was hell. Nobody was allowed to talk about anything or a crew-cut person would come up and smack you in the mouth.

Women were especially cowed by this. We must pity our poor mothers and grandmothers! The crew cuts decreed that they must stay home all day! So women made up the concept of Housework as a total job. Obsessive crazed insane mentally ill anal-compulsive neatness. Neatness that could take an entire day plus a full-time maid to achieve. Today's normal parent lives in a happy clutter of Legos and vomit. But in the fifties a clean house was the only forum for competitive ego satisfaction.

And, what the hell, pity the poor fathers and grandfathers stuck in those gray flannel suits! Work was the new, improved, bloodless warfare. Men were bundles of competitiveness and ego casualties, but could they cry or throw temper tantrums? No. A man's boss would give him the hairy eyeball. The guy would be terrified and ashamed and go home and yell at his wife, the old ball and chain. She would say, "Yes, dear," and bring him a reproachful martini. And the husband would resent the wife's reproach and the wife would resent the husband's crankiness. They would both seethe an uncomprehending, festering, cancer-causing resentment. And then take it out on the kids.

My mother was an hysteric. She had two sisters, also hysterics. These people were not intellectuals. My grandmother had a parakeet named Petey with whom she had long and heartfelt conversations until Petey went cross-eyed from boredom. My Aunt Selma, God rest her soul, ironed her face one day when she thought she was answering the phone. All the aunts had pianos, and on the pianos sat artful groupings of porcelain poodles. And all the cousins took piano lessons from our local sadist and were forced to practice an hour a day, staring furiously at porcelain poodles.

My Aunt Marilyn had a boyfriend who once told me he was going to sneak into my bedroom at night and cut off all my hair. Bastard. I'm still scared of him.

Whenever I saw my grandfather he would grab me and kiss me yuckily and tell me I would grow up and become Miss America. I thought, "Well, maybe." My cousin Ronnie had a plate in his head. My aunts and my grandmother said Ronnie would grow up and become the president of the United States if only all the girls wouldn't kill him by playing like wild Indians around his head. "Stop with the hopscotch!" the aunts would yell in unison. "Your cousin Ronnie has a plate in his head!"

So okay, we were Jews. These women deserved some sympathy. All Jewish women who lived through World War II had every right to be insane, nagging, depressed, wildly overprotective and a veritable cornucopia of convenient maladies and psychoses. For a while anyway. A decade say. I personally think my mother may have been pushing it by going prostrate with severe colitis every time I got a bad report card or was discovered making out with my black boyfriend in the bushes.

Here's what I was taught in the fifties. And when I say taught, I'm not talking about somebody handing me a magazine article every once in a while. I'm talking drummed irrevocably into my head and heart and intestines.

A girl must always be a little lady.

A little lady doesn't yell or act like a wild Indian.

A little lady must always wear a pretty dress, which may never ever get dirty.

So mudpies are completely out.

A little lady must eat everything on her plate because of the starving children in India.

A little lady must never get pudgy or chubby or big-boned or fat or she'll never find a husband.

A little lady must be very very very pretty—pretty enough to be Miss America or at least a ballet dancer, so she can find a husband.

Every little lady must find a husband.

Finding a husband is a little lady's destiny.

So a little lady must be the most popular in school so she can find a husband and fulfill her destiny.

A little lady must not trust other little ladies, who may betray her and step on her head in order to be the most popular and get the best husbands.

A little lady must not make demands or raise her little lady voice or exult in winning.

A little lady must be cute and winsome and ooze adorably around her parents if she wants a new doll or something.

A little lady must be a good listener, laugh at all jokes that the boys make, and imply with all possible body language that the boys are large and in charge. Except for that boy who wants to color with you and play dolls' tea party after school.

When a little lady grows up and finally gets her husband, she will experience the ultimate joy of joys.

And then a little lady will have little children and become a little mother and it will all be pretty aprons and baking cookies and madly happily-ever-after.

I was of course terrified. Every day my mother dressed me for school in my little ladylike clothes and my little barrettes cutting into my little scalp. Every day she admonished me that I'd better be careful or soon she'd have to buy me clothes in the "chubby section." I lived in cold dread of the "chubby section," even though I didn't know what it was, exactly.

Every day I jostled with other little ladies who had been primed by their mothers to exude toxic amounts of sugar and spice and everything nice or else.

Every day we all went to our home economics class. We learned how to skin an orange in one long never-ending peel, and then section the oranges so that they were devoid of pith.

We washed lettuce. We poached eggs. We were given a broom and mop tutorial. We learned how to thread a bobbin and sew an apron and curtains. And just in case, we learned how to type.

And we forced panty girdles onto our eager little prepubescent bodies, which made us very, very angry.

And through it all, we were alone. Not one little lady ever turned to the other little ladies and said, "Fuck this. They can take their perfect angel food cake and shove it up their asses. I'm going fishing."

Until the sixties.

II

DATING GODDAMMIT

4

PROBLEM LADY

Dear Problem Lady:

I forget where we are these days. Is it okay for a woman to ask a man for a date? What's the protocol on this?

What if she asks him and he says no? What if he laughs and says, "Me go out with *you*? You're kidding, right?"

Even worse, what if he says yes?

If she asks him out to dinner does she pay? What if he won't let her? Does she wrestle him to the ground for the check? And if he does let her pay, will it upset his masculinity so that later he won't be able to get it up?

And how does she actually *ask*? Does she use the word "date"? What if that word scares him? But if she doesn't say "date," maybe he'll think that she's just asking him as a friend, and he'll go but nothing will happen, and she won't know what it means and she'll call each of her girlfriends seven times a day to find out what *they* think it means. This could go on for months before she finally realizes that he has no interest in her.

What if he knows it's a date, and he's really excited and he really likes her, and halfway through the evening she discovers he's a yutz and she's made a terrible mistake? How does she let him down without hurting his feelings? And what if he doesn't get the hint and decides he's madly in love with her and starts stalking her so that she has to change her name and move to another town?

And then if things do work out there's the condom thing. Who provides it these days?

You know something? I don't think it's worth it. Do you?

Brenda

Dear Brenda:

You know how you meet a man at a nightclub and borrow somebody's pen and scribble down your number on a napkin shred? When he finds your number two days later he goes through the above thought process. This is the real reason that he never calls you.

This is why more people than ever have taken up good works and left romance behind.

But I say leap. Ask men out with abandon. Not strangers of course. You should have at least one friend in common not only for safety's sake, but for information. You need to know if he's really over his ex-girlfriend, etc.

He'll know it's a date. You really don't have to spell it out. You pay unless he has a fit.

You might get rejected, he may turn out to be a dickhead. But the more you ask men out, the easier it gets, the more powerful you feel, the more chance you have of falling in love.

Just make sure to keep a couple of condoms in your purse.

Oh, and one more thing: You're having a panic attack. You need to breathe into a paper bag or something. Meditate, maybe. Then live in the moment—it's the only place where you can have fun.

Problem Lady

* * *

Dear Problem Lady:

Do you think it's weird to get so happy about a new article of clothing that you burst into tears?

I got the most beautiful jacket, a jacket I never even dreamed could exist, a jacket with a cut that is not in any way derivative but totally creative and also makes me look gorgeous. I took it home, popped it on, stared at myself in the mirror, did a little whirling dervish dance, and felt tears streaming down my face.

Have I gone completely around the bend?

Monica

Dear Monica:

No, you have simply fallen in love. Clothing love, although rare, is very powerful. Also very satisfying, since it never makes you wait by the phone.

Problem Lady

* * *

Dear Problem Lady:

Is it ever okay to break up with someone via answering machine? I mean obviously it's okay if you have some kind of abusive stuff going on or a stalking situation or anything where the other person is obviously a scumbag. And it's not okay if you're about to be married in a week and all the bridesmaids' dresses are ready and waiting to make each participant no matter what body type look like a mushroom. And if you're actually living together the logistics would be tough, unless you have a "memo" feature on your answering machine.

But what about that tricky gray area? What if you've had, say, four dates, you haven't slept together yet, but you can tell the other person is smitten and thinks that now you're in this deeply meaningful long-term relationship? And what if the minute he thought you were in this lovely relationship he felt so relaxed that he just stopped talking?

Which he didn't even notice! I mean, we could easily be walking for a good ten blocks not speaking at all! I would be dredging my brain for something, anything to say that he wouldn't answer with a vague grunt or stark silence:

"Did you like that movie?"

"*(Grunt)*"

"I'm glad it was playing because I really wanted you to see it, it's my favorite movie in the world."

"*(Silence)*"

"Are you hungry?"

"*(Vaguely assenting silence)*"

"What are you in the mood to eat?" (I thought he might have a hearing problem. It can't be a good thing when you suspect your date is deaf.)

"Whatever you want."

"What I want is for you to tell me what you thought of my favorite movie in all the world!" I almost screamed. But instead I gritted my teeth and waited for the end of what I realized would be our very last date.

He called me the next day but I couldn't pick up the phone because I was too pissed off. I realized that was unfair, that he had this John Wayne thing going, and I'm more into a Noël Coward type. But still, I was fuming, I don't know why. So I called him when I knew he was at work and told his machine sorry, but it just wasn't working out for me.

Now I feel so guilty. He thought everything was fine. He must be so hurt.

Melinda

Dear Melinda:

You're pissed off because you're disappointed. You wanted something more than the odd grunt. This is not necessarily a lot to ask.

But in the larger scheme of interpersonal relationships, this guy is not a creep. Possibly paralyzed, possibly passive, possibly just plain tedious, but probably well meaning.

Luckily, you only had a few dates and you never had sex. If you've had more than five dates and/or have had sex with someone it is the rule that you must break up during at least a live phone call, if not in person.

It's better this way. If you actually talked to him, your hostility would start leaking through your well-rehearsed lines.

And what are answering machines for if not to break up with people who bore you?

Problem Lady

* * *

Dear Problem Lady:

I have a date! An actual bona-fide date! A guy who is age-appropriate, intelligent, and has a job and everything. We're going to the theater and then "out for coffee," whatever that means.

"How do you know it's a date?" my friends all asked, because so often someone invites you to a lovely evening activity and you get all excited and lose five pounds and then halfway through the evening you find yourself advising this "date" on how to get his ex-boyfriend back. But I think I'm safe. This guy called, stuttered for five minutes, then said, "I'm really bad at asking women on dates. Will you go out with me?"

Now of course we come to the most grisly, knottiest and mystifying problem plaguing civilization since the beginning of time, baffling experts and turning strong humans into spastic aspic:

What should I wear?

What I'd really like to wear is a fabulous strapless evening gown and tiara. But this may be slightly over-the-top.

A miniskirt with high heels? A TV-anchor red suit? Black deconstructed Japanese chic? Tight jeans and sweater? Floral baby doll? Neosixties? Neoseventies? Neoeighties? Vintage? Spandex? Lace? Leopard print? Leather? *Rubber?*

What I want to convey to him is a woman with confidence, a woman who has her own mind and life, who is sensual yet selective, vulnerable yet strong, who knows how to make seviche if she has to and grow a nice calla lily, who has a brilliant solution to the HMO problem. A woman who is perfect in every way.

What am I going to do? Please help me quick.

Terrorized

Dear Terrorized:

You've run amok with anticipation. I don't care if this is your first date in five years, it's still *just a date*. Things can, and will, go wrong. You'll spill latte down whatever you wear. He'll tell you he just doesn't get Anne Tyler. Dates are about nervous laughter and missed cues. There's nothing you can do to make it right if it's all wrong, hardly any way to ruin it if it's right.

And most times it's wrong. Most times the big momentous date turns into a festival of bad jokes and halitosis, and then two days later you're in a bookstore and trip and fall right into the arms of the love of your life. So calm down already.

And wear whatever you want, barring sweatpants, which double the size of your butt. Do not buy something new. Buying something new is making way too big a deal and tempting the fates.

Wear your favorite outfit. Wear what makes you feel cool and devil-may-care. Do not wear the outfit your friends tell you is fabulous but makes you feel like Cher. Just take a shower, wash your hair, put on your outfit after you've checked it for food spots, pop on a little makeup and a tiny amount of perfume, and relax. Be exactly who you really are.

Or wear the miniskirt and high heels. That always works.

Problem Lady

* * *

Dear Problem Lady:

I think it was while my beloved and I were on vacation in New Orleans and he said he was going out "for lunch" and got back at eight-thirty that I first thought to myself, "I'm piloting this ship alone."

The man is a nightmare. Every day there's another drama, and I myself am not a big drama queen. There was the temper tantrum in The Good Guys when I questioned his VCR purchase. There was the rampant flirting with my accountant. There was a major lie about when he *really* broke up with the ex-girlfriend.

We won't even go into the gift shop incident.

Then last night I had The Dream. There was this great hulking gray guy who was trying to rape me, trying to rob me, yelling at me. Then I was shrieking at my mother. Then I was taking care of two babies. Then this woman in the mirror whispered to me, "I used to go out with him, he's a spoiled brat."

I am not a shrink, although I play one on TV (I'm an actress), but I think I can tell when a dream is holding up a giant billboard saying, "GET OUT NOW! EMERGENCY!"

The guy's got all the annoying characteristics of my mother, he's as much work as two babies, and he's spoiled rotten. I think I should break up with him, don't you?

Trouble is, I love him. Not the bad parts, but the softhearted, vulnerable and brilliant guy that lurks underneath all the bad behavior. I know exactly who he is, even when he's trying to hide it. And in his good moments, he's my best pal. The idea of leaving him fills me with grief.

I have these fantasies about saving him from his own insanity. That's crazy, right? I should get out while I can, right? Okay, then, if you're so smart, tell me how.

Brat Addict

Dear Addict:

Have you thought about animal rescue? Finding homes for needy pups? This may take the edge off your rampant maternal instincts.

"I'm piloting this ship alone" is the operative sentence of your letter. In relationships, you each play Mom or Dad with approximate equality. The whole point is to not feel lonely.

But there's something in this relationship that you can't quite give up. Perhaps it *is* love, pure and simple. Perhaps it's some kind of nasty post-Freudian repetition compulsion. Who the hell cares?

Things will either get better or, way more likely, worse. When the albatross around your neck swells up with gangrene, cross your fingers and flee.

Problem Lady

5

GETTING LAID: THE POINT

IT HAS COME TO MY NOTICE THAT EVERYBODY IN THE WORLD, and I'm including animal and plant species here, does every single thing they do, every toe twitch and eyebrow cock, for one reason and one reason only:

To get laid.

Consider, just for an example, the Monica Lewinsky brouhaha.

It was the best of times, it was the silliest of times. It was the end of January 1998. Every TV station was all-Monica, all-the-time. Anchormen and -women were discussing penile shape, blow jobs and perjury. My phone rang. It was my friend Hank. He was cackling madly.

Originally appeared in *Playboy* magazine.

"This just goes to prove what I've said all along," Hank said. "Never underestimate the Power of the Pussy.

"Think of it. The president of the United States, the most powerful man in the whole world, sees a cute young girl, and he cannot bring himself to walk past her without stopping. To avert an international crisis, all he had to do was keep going."

"Well, you known what they say in Texas," I said. "The trouble with women is they have *all* the pussy."

Later that week I went to my shrink. "Here's what I think," I said. "I think guys want to fuck just about everybody. When a guy says he's not attracted to a woman, all that means is that he wouldn't crawl through two miles of sewer to fuck her. He'd only go half a mile, tops."

"Well," she said pensively, "based on my twenty years of research and experience, I'd say that's pretty much it."

"Fat women?" I asked. "Skinny women, old women, young girls, women with terminal cellulite, women with gigantic hair and tattoos?"

"Don't forget all waitresses," she said.

"Fucking men," I said.

"Why are you feeling that?" she asked, of course.

Because they're sneaky bastards! Because I went through grade school, junior high, high school and decades out in the world before I knew this! Because I have been insecure about my ankles, my tits, my tummy, my nose, my thighs, my fucking eye-fuckingbrows. And my brain. Mainly my brain. I was afraid I was boring them when they looked at me in that slack-jawed way. Now I know it would not matter if I had been reciting multiplication tables. Now I know they were just picturing me naked.

Pisses me off.

And meanwhile, guys have spent too many years wondering if women liked them, if women wanted to sleep with them, worrying that maybe they would never, ever get to touch *it* again.

For all you guys out there who are in an agony of insecurity, I have something very, very important to say to you.

Keep worrying.

Women are really picky! One tiny little thing, like a pen protector or an ascot (definitely an ascot), can turn a woman off forever!

This does not mean that women have less interest in getting laid. Pretty much everything a woman does is in the service of finding a man she wants to fuck. The salad eating. The agonizing over paint chips. The face cream. The improving books. The air-popped corn. All details are crucial, including nail color (French manicure? pink for innocent? red for sexy? blue for mentally ill? matte? metallic?). Because once a woman finds a man she really wants to fuck, she wants to keep him around. This is the hard part. This is the part that makes us buy "self-help" books by the stunningly moronic and evil Dr. Laura.

The only time women are not trolling for the ultimate cosmic fuck of their entire lives is when they go to flea markets or antique fairs. The purpose of flea markets and antique fairs is to let a woman stroll hither and thither without having to hold her stomach in.

The crucial truth is that the reason for every human's existence is to get laid as much as possible. Our bodies are simply vessels for our nasty greedy genes that want to trample everybody else's genes under their tiny gene feet. (Read *The Selfish*

Gene, by Richard Dawkins, and you'll see I'm right, except for genes having feet.)

If one takes existence down to this elemental floor, one can see why certain really annoying human patterns emerge.

Who seems to have built all the buildings, composed all the music, painted all the art, figured out carburetors, dug gold mines? Fucking men, that's who. Why? Because they wanted to get laid. Rock-and-roll stars? As Robbie Robertson said in *The Last Waltz,* they were in it for the pussy. You think Michelangelo painted the Sistine Chapel out of religious feeling? Please. You think David E. Kelley writes seventeen different TV series every season because he enjoys hanging with network execs? He knew it would be the only way to get Michelle Pfeiffer into bed.

Where does that leave us women? Screwed, of course. I'm not even going to go into the famous patriarchy, with its women-as-chattel-who-are not-even-permitted-to-learn-to-read-let-alone-have-property agenda. Fuck that, we're not there anymore. What about the fact that every time a woman writes a poem or builds an airplane men give her the hairy eyeball? Women lawyers, doctors and chief executives are, on a daily basis, knocked out of the way as men stampede toward cocktail waitresses.

Women become intellectual and powerful in spite of the fact that it massively lowers their chances of getting laid. This is so heroic and brave and unfair that sometimes we get despondent.

So we really enjoy a good ironic laugh.

A man works as hard as he can, steps on other men's heads, pulls himself up by any bootstrap he can find so that he can have as many women as possible. If he's really, really, really, really good at it, maybe he gets to be the president of the United States.

Which means he is the alpha male of the whole human pack. His genes are raring to go, demanding to multiply.

If he doesn't go after every girlish intern who bats her eyelashes at him, he is clearly out of his mind. Would we want a crazy man with an entire military complex at his disposal?

God only knows what's going on in the White House now with hypocrites helming. And in every government mansion, every corporation president's inner office, every single rock-and-roll tour bus all over the land. Right now eyelashes are being batted, skirts are being lifted.

Propagation of the species, baby.

6

DATER BEWARE

EVEN IF YOU'VE NEVER BEEN A WOMAN WHO LOVES MEN who hate women too much, even if you have no fears of intimacy or boundary issues or any garden-variety neurosis at all (haha), there are certain men who can ruin your life and make you decide that the best look for you is a lovely wimple.

Sometimes it's hard to tell until it's too late. Here we will cover a few of the most obvious problem dates, although there are always new and deadly mutations. So watch it.

IFFY MEN

These are men with just a whisper of something askew that needs to be carefully evaluated. Like, oh, maybe he worships Satan. Do not, at your peril, neglect the following warning signs:

He calls you a "classy lady," a "special lady" or a "special classy lady."

He visibly needs dental work.

He doesn't have a dog because it is "too much responsibility."

He still has his ex's makeup stashed somewhere in his bathroom.

He swears he only watches PBS.

He can't eat unless his napkin is folded like a swan.

He uses the adjective "delicious" to describe people, not cake.

He paints stripes on his face prior to attending sporting events.

He wears fur.

He wears tight pants. Or leather pants. Or tight leather pants.

He sports visible hairplugs or even wears an actual hairpiece, which is only okay if he's an actor.

He's an actor.

He suggests candlelit dinners, long walks on the beach, and describes himself as "youthful," or exhibits other behavior that suggests he's Mr. Personal Ad.

He's bald, yet he has a ponytail.

He's over thirty, yet he has a ponytail.

He's a stockbroker, yet he has a ponytail.

He is clean-shaven, except for a horrid little tuft of hair right above his chin.

He really loves his mother.

He really hates his mother.

He wears Italian loafers without socks.

He remembers and tells you his SAT scores.

His checks have a pastel background of kitties playing with yarn.

You may think, "Oh, so what, his pants are tight," or even "Why should I care if he's missing a front tooth?" Yet these little traits are simply the tip of a big personality iceberg: A man who is afraid of the responsibility of a dog will most likely leave you out in the rain. A stockbroker with a ponytail has a yen to be involved in organized crime. A man who says he only watches PBS usually suffers from herpes. Always remember: If she is anywhere, God is in the details.

On the other hand, there are geeks out there, and they, as geeks, have no social skills at all and would have fared way better had they been brought up by wolves. It is totally possible for a geek—anyone who has ever, in any sense, written "code"—to exhibit all the traits listed above and still be perfectly fine, since he simply read the wrong "how to be a human" manual and can be easily led away from the Sansabelt slacks with a judicious cattle prod.

ARE YOU READY FOR THE "/" GUYS?

There is something very swoony about the "/" guys. You know, the carpenter/musician, the housepainter/sculptor, the dentist/photographer. This guy exudes a certain brooding poetry, a vulnerability, and a disarming zest for sex anywhere and anytime, including fields and stairwells. And he'll write a song about you, because even if a "/" guy is a plumber/poet, he still plays the guitar. They all play the guitar. Accoustic. Without such guys, no women in NYC would have had a date for the past three decades.

Our "/" guy will thrill us when in his twenties and early thirties. But he will undoubtedly not be so cute in his forties and fifties, when he will still be wandering around vaguely with plaster in his hair, clutching his beloved fifty-year-old Gibson guitar. It is the law that when a "/" guy hits forty-five, he must move to Berkeley or Austin, Texas, and smoke pot until he dies.

Yes, our "/" guy does have the capacity to form a permanent pair bond, although he will never actually mature. You will be supporting him. You will also spend an awful lot of time listening to him pick out Richard Thompson tunes on the guitar, bobbing your head, snapping your fingers and closing your eyes in perfect bliss, even though you're secretly thinking about handbags.

I myself have spent approximately three decades sitting on sofas, smiling with a bright rictus of appreciation while assorted men serenaded me. There was a huge parade of them—junkies, accountants, editors, plumbers, even actual card-carrying musicians. One thing went through my mind the whole time: Stop playing already! I really only wanted to joke and make out.

The scariest guy like this I've ever met was a carpenter/professional storyteller. This guy is in his fifties, lives in Berkeley, has a wife and three children. His wife supports them, even with all the carpentry/professional storytelling. Every Christmas he buys her Birkenstocks. The scariest part: All their children are SINGER/SONGWRITERS! This woman always looks just a tad glazed, as if she's on a full-spectrum antidepressant cocktail. I believe the only reason she hasn't killed herself yet is that she is just too tired.

ESCHEW THE RENAISSANCE MAN!

Still a "/" guy has a certain charm, unlike the dreaded Renaissance man. I forbid you to go out with this guy. I forbid you to even ask him for directions. Any fellow who defines himself as a Renaissance man is telling you, in shorthand, "I am full of a quiet yet all-encompassing knowledge and no matter what you know, I will always know better than you and will chuckle with a quiet condescension whenever you challenge me and I might even smoke a pipe. Plus, I don't make any money ever, but that is not my fault. It is the fault of the system."

You may think *your* Renaissance man is not like this. But they are all like this. The underlying theme of the Renaissance man is that his entitlement expectations are off the chart.

Once when I was working on a sitcom my friend Marco and I went out to dinner with Meg, an actress, and Brad, her R.m. husband. We were talking, as all sitcom writers will whenever they can open their mouths, about the stupidity of the networks, how no good sitcom goes unpunished, etc. Brad looked at us pityingly.

"We need to find a way to liberate the sitcom from television. We can do sitcoms in the park if we have to! In fact, I already have a project to do sitcoms in the park. A lot of the more edgy producers who have been burned by Hollywood are interested. If it's good, and of course it will be good, people will come. Interested?"

Oh yeah, we were interested. Interested in checking him into the nearest NUTHOUSE.

"Brad is such a Renaissance man," Meg said fondly. She is no longer with him. She is now—I swear this is true—with a Baldwin brother.

REALLY BAD IDEAS

I'm sure everyone knows this but, just in case, do not decide that any of the following could be kinda maybe okay if only you could change them a little bit, or maybe if they had a good woman's love:

Convicted felons are never appropriate. God only knows what they got up to in jail. Yes, drug dealers and inside traders do fall into this category. Even if we ignore any morality in making a decision, these guys' lives are way too big and unwieldy. They'll never fold the laundry.

Also, while it may be true that, as a group, serial killers are better-looking than your average man, hell, some of them are dishy, do not decide to become engaged to one.

Warning signs that your date is a serial killer:

1. Hates animals.
2. Antisocial.
3. Stringy hair.
4. Eyes snap open in the middle of the night.
5. Not on a bowling team.
6. Often really cranky.

Almost as bad as serial killers are:

Married Men

Unless of course you're also married, in which case you suck for cheating on your husband. Leave him and get it over with. But if you are single, it is NEVER appropriate to date a married man because:

1. He's cheating on her, he'll cheat on you.
2. You only *think* you're seeing his real personality.
3. He's a big liar and is morally flawed.
4. You'll be a bit player in someone else's soap opera.
5. He'll have plenty of them, but no excuse for why he's married to someone else is ever really true. He's married to someone else because he wants to be.
6. Don't be a sap.

And this I can say with the utmost authority in the world. Beware of:

Men Who Are Out of Their Fucking Minds

All of them. No exceptions. You really wouldn't be happy with the guy in *Cuckoo's Nest.*

You especially want to stay away from guys with borderline personality disorder, suicidal tendencies, even a *tad* of schizophrenia. No funny lovely manic-depressives. No adorable damaged narcissists. Okay, maybe a damaged narcissist or there will be no one at all.

But make it your code never to date anyone more mentally ill than you are.

And, finally,

The Addicts

Here's why you should never date anyone who is an alcoholic, a drug addict, a big ole gambler or a huffer of glue:

Because, no matter what, he will break your heart.

Contrary to movies of the week, most addicts do not look or act like psychotic mass murderers with Bell's palsy. Your basic addict is not a bad person but is, in fact, too fucking charming. He's sweet, intuitive, pretty and he gives incredible head, since an addict is sensitive, he feels things deeply, he is all exposed nerve endings and empathy.

If he walks down the street and sees a lonely soldier sitting on a stoop, he doesn't just walk on by. No way. He walks on by with his heart breaking, goes home and writes a song about a lonely soldier sitting on a stoop watching a fellow walk by. Everything hurts all the time if you're an addict.

I once knew a singer/songwriter who wrote songs that were exquisite mixtures of hilarity and pain, including a song about a soldier sitting on a stoop watching a fellow walk by. We did more drugs than I have even *seen* since. Jeez, those were the fucking days.

But it didn't mean anything because he had a girlfriend back at home to whom he was being unfaithful. The drugs I took made it easy to be in total denial of this. I tried to believe we had something because we joked and laughed and the whole band became my friends and I got to sit backstage in my fishnet stockings.

But one time we were at a hotel, sitting on the floor, he was talking on the phone. He reached out, took my leg in his hand, stroking the stubbles on my calf with absentminded tenderness. The sweetness of the moment overwhelmed me then, it overwhelms me now. It was just a random gesture, but I was so hopelessly hungry for sweet affection that I tried to get same from a womanizing unavailable drunk singer/songwriter. When that happened, I knew for sure that I was fucking doomed.

Not all singer/songwriters are alcoholics, but all alcoholics think they are singer/songwriters.

Hell, just stay away from anyone who makes you chronically unhappy.

And always remember, it is way, way better to be unhappy on your own than to be unhappy with some loon.

7

THE ALLEGED SHAME OF SOLO

I'M FEELING LIKE A BIG JERK.

You know how when you go totally mental with hatred toward someone but you cannot really articulate why? She hasn't stolen your dress or your job, she has not been mean to animals or even a shrub, but you just want her dead?

This probably means one of three things about this human:

1. She reminds you of your mother.
2. She reminds you of some aspect of yourself that makes you want to puke.
3. She is a space alien serial killer.

I have been wondering why a fairly bland woman named Ann has driven me insane with fury. All she did was say she never is lonely, she loves her life and has a fulfilling relationship with all her friends, and if romance came along, well, fine, but she wasn't holding her breath.

Wait, you hate her too? Why? Is it that she's lying? Or what? Why do I need to go straight for her throat? I'm trying to figure it out.

Some of you who know me might remember that once, in a galaxy far away, I was desperate for a boyfriend. Every hour on the hour the evil mommy in my head would pipe up, "You're alone! You'll always be alone! You suck! If you try getting close to a guy, he's gonna notice not only your thighs, not only your upper arms, but also your loathsome disgusting neediness, your halitosis of the brain, your pitiful facade of being a normal, everyday girl, you fucking freak."

Yes, I thought I was empty without a man. A fucking fish that needed a goddamned bicycle. For a feminist, this is a serious emotional glitch.

Coupled with the absolutely reptilian need to get laid, this glitch meant great big trouble.

I would fuck someone, and the evil mommy voice would make me believe I was in love, even though the guy was a cocaine addict ex-con with "love" and "hate" tattooed on his knuckles. Then the voice, which lacked even rudimentary self-esteem, would tell me I wasn't good enough for him. Then I'd twist myself into a pretzel of what I hoped was feminine cuteness, complete with garter belts and giggles, but somehow I could never make it work with the ex-con cocaine addict and therefore it was all too true, I was the lowest of worms. I couldn't keep a man. I sucked. The shame of being solo would hit me like a ton of self-help books.

Naturally I was teeming with a huge jealous resentment of anybody who had any sort of relationship. Especially my friends with mates who had the fucking nerve to smile at me, the bastards.

I knew what that smile said. That smile said, "Hahaha! I am smiling smugly because I have a man and you don't! I am now going to tell you that it's no big deal having a man! I'll act all surprised that you might think it's important, but I'm lying! See how I smile pityingly while I lie? I got myself some homegrown dick and you don't!"

This was a very articulate smile my friends were smiling, and I knew they were doing this because on the occasions when I had a boyfriend, especially when I had a hot sex big penis boyfriend, I would get this warm, delicious relief plus a noxious smugness in my heart, and I would smile in just the same way.

Which makes me the biggest jerk alive. I don't believe I'm the only one. Many of us wear our men as proudly as Girl Scout badges. My shrink relayed to me that she joined a gym and met a group of women in the locker room. Within *five minutes,* each woman made her male attachment parts known to the group.

"My husband will kill me if I'm late tonight."

"Oh, my boyfriend gets jealous about other guys, even at the gym!"

My husband . . . my boyfriend . . . my sweetie, my beloved, my dude. It reminds me of men comparing their cars, or girlfriends.

And it's enough to make you feel really uneasy when you're alone.

When I didn't have a man, I would pretend that I didn't care, that everything was just peachy as hell. And that's why I hated Ann. She was lying in just the same way I had been known to, oozing with shame about her rampant neediness, and pretending it wasn't there. I knew it was. We were having lunch. I said to her, "There's nothing worse than a woman who is alone and feels really disgustingly desperate about it and won't admit it. You are exuding a stench of shame when there's nothing to be ashamed about, you idiot."

"Check, please," said Ann to the waitress.

You think I had a few projection issues, maybe? "Oh my God, I am SO sorry," I said to Ann's back. "That was totally evil and uncalled-for."

Too damned many of us who are alone feel so ridiculously all grim and secretive about our loneliness.

How the hell can we not? Every fucking minute there is an article in *TV Guide* about some poor, beleaguered dramatic-series star who has recently broken up with her husband and she is so *wounded,* so resolutely brave in the face of the awful tragedy that has struck her life that it's amazing she doesn't just swallow hemlock and get it over with.

But what's even worse, if you ask me, are the women's magazines' "Joys of Singlehood"–type pieces. You know, the ones made up of lists that say that single women:

1. Can eat anything! Whenever we like! No pesky mealtimes!
2. Eat cake icing right out of the can! With our *fingers!*
3. Make a horrible unsightly mess anywhere in the

house with no one to see! Five-day-old sandwiches and everything!

4. Walk around all naked! Nobody can see hideous cellulite! Never again have to shave legs!
5. Say good-bye to contact lenses! Panty hose! Hot rollers! Toothpaste!
6. Say hello to incessant farting!
7. Have a vibrator that always works, doesn't need beer!

These stories always end up with our narrator having an epiphany. She always dreaded being alone, but it wasn't bad! It was good! Now she was all spiritual and in tune with lunar cycles and the earth mother! Or else she was plucky! Plucky, forsooth!

Naturally these passive-aggressive stories give me The Panic. I'll be sitting around, reading a nice fashion magazine, and read a piece called, maybe, "Alone! But Not Lonely!" and a grave anxiety will grip my stomach and I'll feel as if I'm hurtling into space. Is it just me?

No. It's another goddamn plot by big corporations to make us buy things that promise to make us prettier, thinner, younger, glossier, smarter, exude crucial pheromones, eradicate self-loathing and generally become as catnip to all possible sex partners. At least.

So they shame us. Overtly and covertly there are huge giant messages in movies and magazines and newscasts and everywhere that women in our society must attach themselves to a big strong penis or, what the hell, any penis at all.

It is constant pernicious propaganda! And it is aimed mainly at women. An article about the single male soap star in *TV Guide* will generally just say, "Guess what, girls? He's available!" Probably because men, no matter how unattractive they feel, will buy a set of lug wrenches before they would fork out even a dime for tinted SPF 30 moisturizer.

But single women are portrayed as something akin to flesh-eating bacteria. We read those articles, especially the perky, plucky, allegedly upbeat ones, and we feel that if we don't have a resident penis, we must kill ourselves immediately.

And (news flash!) the bastards are telling us exactly the opposite of the truth and don't want us to notice. People are always doing this, you have to watch them like a Border collie. The more they try to convince us of something, the more they are secretly afraid that the opposite is true. For example, I believe that it is only born-again Christians who are the atheists in the foxholes.

Who benefits most from the traditionally roled marriage/partnership thing?

You'd think after reading those articles, seeing the movies and breathing in propaganda that it would be women, right? But what about all the studies that show single women and married men as much happier than married women and single men? I'm going to go way out on a limb here and say that it's always been men who benefited most from marriage, from the olden times until about, oh, two years ago when things started getting better, possibly coinciding with the time when the sons and daughters of early feminists became grown-ups.

Of course it's only been a short time that women had the right not to be married. There were those pesky women-as-chattel days, there were the virginity-until-marriage rules and then the women-are-too-soppy-and-stupid-to-be-businessmen times.

There were always hindrances, but if one could get around them, one could be very happy indeed without a lord and master. One could live in a little cottage in Oxfordshire and be constantly found in strange gardening hats deadheading roses and chatting cozily with one's female companion.

Now, finally, most of the hindrances are gone, there is less financial hardship in being single, and singlehood is a valid "lifestyle" choice. But the brides' magazines get bigger and bigger, celebrity weddings are huge, and the propaganda machine is running overtime to keep us panting after matrimony.

So we should laugh, ha! ha! ha!, at this propaganda, but not all of us do. Instead we become despondent and fall into their evil plots, buying crazy cellulite creams and scented aromatherapeutic cuticle softeners.

We don't have to do this! We can say "TCHAH!" and "Nerts!" and "Blow me!" to the cruel and unusual society-produced shame about being alone. We can throw off the stigma of solo! We can snap our fingers playfully and possibly even poke at the eyes of those who imply there is something wrong with us if we don't have men!

Then, and only then, will we be able to feel our own unfettered loneliness and look it squarely in the eyeball.

THERE IS NO SHAME IN BEING LONELY! WE ARE ALLOWED TO WANT A MATE! A MATE IS A GOOD THING IF HE OR SHE IS NOT PLAGUED WITH PESKY BORDERLINE PERSONALITY DISORDER!

What happens when a guy says he is lonely? Is he shunned or shamed? No! He is inundated with casseroles! Everyone wants to take care of him!

Not only that, but guys are always breaking dates with other guys to go out with a love opportunity. The other guys never care about this. They do not say, "You are woman-centered and how dare you?" They say, "You bastard! Does she have a friend?" And because men don't have the history of being told they are the less important sex, the breaking of a movie date with another guy is not weighted with thousands of years of the oppression, belittlement, marginalization and rampant ridicule that women have experienced. Guys never felt they were simply a place mark and less important.

It is all so very unfair that guys don't have this guilt and shame, goddamn them. But I am not blaming guys. I like guys. Especially the guys running around these days, who often notice these injustices themselves.

Women, however, after the empowerment of the sisterhood, feel it's important not to let down the side, so we feel guilt at the very *thought* of canceling a date with other women. But why? We've come such a long way, we should be allowed to blow each other off without it becoming a huge *issue* full of even more shame.

It's the shame that will make you sick and full of self-loathing. Own your loneliness. Share your loneliness with others. Bring your desperation in from out of the cold. If you do this, your self-esteem won't let you believe that you are really in love with ex-cons with love and hate tattooed on their knuckles.

If you do this, you will be able to discern the difference between being in love and simply getting laid.

If I do this, I will stop feeling vitriolic toward Ann. I will feel empathy and understanding about her not admitting her loneliness and will hate her instead for her fringed boots.

Say it now, I'M LONELY AND I'M PROUD! I AM SICK WITH HORNINESS AND I VOTE!

Say it enough and the bad mojo of even a thousand *TV Guide* stories of bereft starlets will cause you not a whit of uneasiness and you will be FREE!

III

RELATIONSHIPS AND BREAKDOWNS

8

PROBLEM LADY

Dear Problem Lady:

I'm having a little trouble picking up the phone when it rings. I just know it's going to be some idiot wanting me to work or some friend wanting to talk relationships. So I haven't really answered the phone much in a month. Well, two months. Also I don't like to go out much. I used to go to the post office, no problem. Now it seems like a really lame idea. Ditto the coffee shop. Why go out when they deliver?

The coffee shop guy talked to me the other day. He said, "You've been wearing the same nightgown all week." Before that I didn't know he had a voice.

Then he stopped by yesterday when I hadn't ordered any food, wanting to know how I am. "I'm fine," I said.

"Maybe a little soup?" he asked.

"Not hungry," I said. He stared at me for a minute and went away.

Today he came back with a booklet from the drugstore called *Depression and You.*

I used to think this guy was cute, but now he's working my nerves. I read the booklet. I'm not depressed. Depressed people are sad and full of self-loathing. I loathe others. I have no feelings at all.

How can I get the coffee shop guy to leave me alone? How can I get all guys to leave me alone?

Susan

Dear Susan:

Of course you're depressed. You're so depressed you've shut down completely, although a little anger is shining through. I'm thinking it's relationship trouble. Probably you go for grungy, withholding musicians, but perhaps I'm projecting.

So here's what I order you to do: Go to the movies with the coffee shop guy. This is one sweet, perceptive fellow. This is a fellow who, if this were a movie, you'd marry in the third act. And at this point in your depression any movement at all will be good. Get him to take you to a sad movie, some equivalent to *Terms of Endearment*. You need to cry.

Find out if he has a wife. If he doesn't, kiss him good-night.

Problem Lady

* * *

Dear Problem Lady:

Is there any surefire way to tell if a man is gay? Besides asking him, I mean.

Sometimes I meet a clearly gay man at a party and I'm about to start calling him girlfriend when out of nowhere he'll beckon over a woman and baby whom he introduces as his family. I remember the first time this happened.

"This is my wife, Tiffany, and my baby, Jared," said the gay man.

"Oh, girleen you are so droll," I answered.

It didn't go over the way I'd hoped. A certain frigid atmosphere took over. The guy was obviously *deeply* closeted.

It's happened so often lately I've lost confidence. A guy I still swear was wearing eye shadow introduced me to his wife, twins, *and* mother-in-law.

Okay, so a lot of men are trying to be straight. I can understand. I despise them for it, but I understand. Fear turns us perverted.

Anyway, with all these pretenders running around, how do I make sure of a welcome for some nice, wholesome flirting?

Marc

Dear Marc:

After doing extensive research and much fieldwork, I have discovered a surefire way to determine gayness in men.

What you do is walk up to the guy in question and say, "You wouldn't be doing this to me if I weren't in this chair."

If the guy right away says, "But you are, Blanche, you are," he's gay. Extra points for a southern accent.

Problem Lady

* * *

Dear Problem Lady:

I hope that you are well and happy and that all your hopes and dreams come true.

Wait a minute! It's funny that I felt compelled to write the above sentence, because that's the gist of my problem! I have a friend whose hopes and dreams have come true, the *bitch.*

Susie's fallen in love, thank you very much, and so the stars must treble in the skies, birds must soar in unison, the world must reverse on its axis. Susie's in fucking love.

I'm not bitter, I know I sound it, but I'm not. If fact, I'm only pretending this happened to my friend. There is no Susie. It's really me who has fallen in love and *I am so deliriously happy!!! I never knew life could be like this!!!!!!!!!!*

Oh, okay, it's not me, really, it is Susie. I just thought I'd try those sentences on for size. I find them just as annoying as I thought I would.

I admit Susie doesn't actually say these things. God no, that would be too simple. Susie's basic motif is, "Oh, Jesus what am I doing what's the point I know how these things end but on the other hand why not live your life instead of protecting yourself from pain and confusion wait a minute on the other hand I was perfectly happy before having a fine life thank you no man that I cared too much about but a great job and wonderful friends and my cats and all no no no that's wrong I have a whole new dimension in my life now and I don't want it to go away and as we all know I have abandonment issues and so therefore I'm screwed I know that I am totally screwed do you think I'm screwed?"

This conversational method, especially when repeated ad infinitum, is not enough to keep the mind alive. I have had patience, I have had forbearance, I have listened to more hours of "so then he said . . . so then I said . . . and my shrink says . . ." than is healthy for any normal woman, let alone me with hypoglycemia.

But really, what's the point? I may not be bitter (and *okay*, goddammit, the state of my goddamned bitterness may be in question here), but I am definitely jealous. And lonely. It's not nearly as much fun having your traditional Sunday breakfast of popovers and strawberry butter with your best friend when suddenly there's this hulking masculine presence at the table, and this h.m.p. is showering Susie with feathery kisses and calling her "sugar plum." It kind of takes the zest out of any gossip I may have about Maggie and her new riding instructor. Therefore *I'm* the one with problems, Susie's the one who's happy and getting laid, yet I'm supposed to just be this listening machine.

So I don't think it's fair that she got all red in the face and told me she would never speak to me again just because I mentioned to her that I'm feeling this way. She says I'm a bad friend. Hah!

I think I'm the one who needs solace and support. I think *she's* the one who is a bad friend.

Don't you think?

Margot

Dear Margot:

Let me just say very quickly that it is extremely bad form on Susie's part to bring any presence, hulking or otherwise, to something as sacred as a traditional Sunday breakfast between girlfriends. No one should be allowed to do this without imprisonment, fine, or both.

It is also desirable for the friend of the first part to monitor her conversations somewhat, to notice when her incoherent ramblings are on the verge of turning the friend of the second part's brain into resentful Jell-O, no matter how much pain the friend of the first part is experiencing.

That's right, I said *pain*. You think your friend is on some kind of picnic of frivolity? Did you or did you not see *Moonstruck* where Nicolas Cage stands in the snow and explains fully just how dire the consequences are those of falling in love?

Falling in love, while it has its heady moments, also has a full supply of fear and dread. There you are, living your life, minding your own business, and suddenly you're in a train wreck. Everything is turned inside out and backwards, all your priorities and peace of mind are scrambled. Your heart is singing a bright new song, you're walking on clouds of air, then you trip over a curb and knock yourself unconscious. That is love.

Try and remember this is miserable for you, but horrible for Susie. The nutritional aspects alone (not eating, eating everything in sight, throwing up) are making her a basket case. And then there's the sleep deprivation. And the utter terror.

Make peace with her, even though she's being an obnoxious cow.

Problem Lady

* * *

Dear Problem Lady:

I found out my boyfriend cheated on me.

Don't you love that sentence? Just a few common, everyday, banal words. Words that make my heart break into one zillion pieces. My boyfriend cheated on me. I still can't believe it.

Naturally I broke up with him.

I started dating Rupert on October 20 and started sleeping with him on October 21. I am not smart but I am horny. On October 27 I clearly remember asking him, "Are you seeing anyone else?" and he clearly said "No." Then I told him he had to tell me if he did start seeing anyone else because I'm not cut out for such hijinks. (I just think why play games? Why pretend to be cool and uninterested when anyone smarter than a banana slug can read my body language in one nanosecond and tell I'm smitten.)

So then I regretfully went away on business for a few weeks, reading Rupert's horoscope every day and waking up every morning with memories of Rupert coursing through my groin.

Yet, funnily enough, during this time, Rupert started fooling around with some bitch. I mean I know she's not a bitch, but she's a bitch if you see what I mean. They saw each other for two weeks, I came home, he saw her a few more times. Fine, you say? What if I told you while I was away Rupert told me he loved me? Is that nice?

So now here we are in March. I just found out, it's not interesting how. Rupert is devastated and, well, a little hysterical. He keeps saying, "It was the beginning of the relationship. I didn't know where we stood. Don't you realize I stopped seeing her because of you?" Like I'm supposed to be flattered.

Here's what I need to know. Why does Rupert think what he did wasn't so bad?

Also, should I go back to him?

Gwen

Dear Gwen:

On your behalf I just did a poll of every monogamous man who would pick up his phone. Sit down. The results may shock you. They certainly shocked me.

Every last one of them thought this behavior was okay.

"The beginning? The beginning never counts," said Stephen.

"Yeah, it's even okay to lie in the beginning," said Paul.

"That real early stuff doesn't count at all," said my actual son.

These are not rock musicians or movie producers or pricks with ponytails. These are guys that are faithful and trustworthy.

Yet when I called the usual female suspects, they were livid and wanted the guy's head on a plate.

So what we have here is another failure to communicate. Guys have neglected to tell us some secret guy code. You can only believe them after a certain, unspecified amount of time.

"Like a month," my son said.

"A couple of months or so," said Rob.

"Who the hell knows?" said James.

So here's an idea. Don't sleep with a guy until you're pretty positive you can trust him.

Yeah, right.

Should you go back with someone named Rupert? I would normally say yes, except he did say he loved you and while he was seeing someone else.

This, even by guy standards, is careless behavior.

Problem Lady

* * *

Dear Problem Lady:

Suddenly out of nowhere Bill's and my sex life has been almost nonexistent, like once a month if I'm lucky. Before we were a three-times-a-week kind of couple. Something was wrong.

And yet everything seemed right. Bill was in great spirits, joking, getting his laundry done, buying me flowers and a Dustbuster. He seemed optimistic and positive, a big improvement on his usual curmudgeonly self.

I was baffled, confused, a-twitter. I thought maybe he was having an affair. I followed him around one afternoon for a couple of minutes but then I thought, "What kind of paranoid moron follows her boyfriend around?" So I gritted my teeth and asked him what was what.

He's on antidepressants! He was embarrassed and trying to work up the nerve to tell me. His shrink gave them to him and mentioned they might affect his libido, but Bill hadn't noticed that they did. So I have two questions.

Do I want a boyfriend who's on antidepressants?

How do I get our sex life back?

Marjorie

Dear Marjorie:

A boyfriend who is on antidepressants is a boyfriend who is in touch with his feelings enough to know he doesn't want to have them anymore.

This is an improvement on many men, who wouldn't recognize depression if it wore a name tag and bit them on the ankle.

On the other hand, a girl wants to get laid.

They have a ton of new antidepressants now, and a person is hardly depressed if he's not on a cocktail of two or three kinds of drugs. For example:

1. Paxil as an antidepressant.
2. Wellbutrin to alleviate impotence problems and sugar craving problems caused by Paxil.
3. BuSpar to curtail anxiety.

Ask him to ask his psychopharmacologist to get modern.

If this doesn't help, go to your nearest sex toy store and buy yourself a Rabbit Pearl, which is a vibrating pink jelly penis with a differently vibrating bunny sitting on top. This is a very charming *objet*. You and your boyfriend will have a lot of fun playing with it.

Problem Lady

* * *

Dear Problem Lady:

I'm a very lonely guy, I'm hopeless with women, and now this great woman is coming on to me. She's sweet, cute, witty, self-deprecating. I can talk to her without feeling like the biggest dork in the world.

Thing is, she's got a kid. Now, I like kids. Kids are great. I even want kids someday. But not now. I'm a young guy, someday I'll be ready for that kind of responsibility, but at twenty-five I feel like a little kid myself.

I'm having a really hard time pulling away from this goddess, but I think I should, don't you? I mean, she should have someone who's ready.

Mark

Dear Mark:

That is one of the most imaginative rationalizations for not getting involved I've heard in a long time.

What is it with you guys? You project so far into the future that a girl gives you a come-hither glance and you've got yourself married, working in a bank, living in the suburbs and coaching Little League. And then you panic and run away, while the girl broods and wonders if she had spinach in her teeth or what, never realizing that you had already planned the purchase of joint burial plots.

Have you ever heard of taking things one step at a time? Seeing how things go? Letting things take their natural course?

I mean, did this woman ask you to take care of her? What makes you think she wants you to? Maybe she can take care of herself very well, thank you. Maybe she likes the responsibility and doesn't plan to hand it over to anyone in the near or far future?

Stop being so conventional and go for it, you fool.

Problem Lady

* * *

Dear Problem Lady:

How can I tell if my feelings are real or if I'm just being neurotic?

I'm probably just being neurotic. It's like those incredibly intricate and involved fungus plants that you'd swear were roses or dandelions or apples or even birds because they're so detailed and real-looking, but they're only fungus.

That's me and my love life. I notice a guy, maybe I make a few vague little jaunts in his direction just in case he likes me but usually I think, Oh what's the use he's too cute and cool he'll think I'm a big dork.

But say I do make a jaunt. Half the time it's a totally useless jaunt and the guy is completely uninterested in me. And even if I've hardly expended any effort at all, even if I've just said, "Want to get some coffee or something?" and he doesn't respond, I have to go to bed for two weeks.

But say the jaunt pays off and the guy responds. Then I get all wired and overexcited and nervous and can't think of anything except "Is this the one? Will this be the guy for me?" and I laugh too much at his jokes and call him at 3:00 A.M. and hang up when he answers. And half the time this kind of behavior turns the guy off after two or three dates. So then I have to go to bed for a month.

But sometimes the guy really does stick around, even when I'm being a trying-too-hard, wearing-too-much-mascara and laughing-too-much dork. And then it's all very magical and fabulous and so romantic that we might as well be moving in slow motion with violins in the background.

And it goes on and I'm thrilled but then I see *The Look*. We'll be walking down the street eating ice cream cones and laughing maybe and then I'll notice this soppy look on his face and my blood will turn to ice. The Look is all soft and runny and weak and worshipful, and it's really annoying. It means I found yet another sap who will put up with anything and let me walk all over him. I hate The Look.

But even then I still have hope. Maybe it wasn't The Look at all, maybe the guy was coming down with a virus or something. So I try to pull away a little, and hope things get better.

They never do! They get worse! I start getting demands. I start getting "I love you, what's the matter why are you pulling away from me?" I'm the one getting the calls at 3:00 A.M.

So then I have to do the "It's not you, it's me" thing. And then run away as fast as I can.

What is wrong with me? Why do I only attract these weak, sappy guys? Why are my instincts so completely fucked up? Why am I so neurotic I can only find pathetic saps to love me?

Debbie

Dear Debbie:

Thank you so much. Yours was a very enlightening, fascinating letter. You have detailed for us beautifully the workings of the mind of a villainous scourge.

All over the world people are grabbing their heads and moaning over people like you. Women in Spain are saying (in Spanish) to their girlfriends, "He just kept coming after me, I thought he was really in love with me, but the minute I responded he dumped me. What's the matter with me?" Men in New Zealand are clutching their balls and muttering, "What the fuck just happened?"

You know that *Look* you so revile? That isn't a look of weakness or sappiness, that is a look of love and trust. That is the look of a person who has finally decided to let down their defenses against getting hurt. That is a look of someone who can bear to let someone get close to them.

I want to write all kinds of nice nourishing things to you, showing you that it isn't so awful letting people get near you, asking you if you had an overbearing, overly controlling parent who never let you alone to grow and flower in your own special way. A parent who never respected your boundaries and made you into a craven, furtive, sad, and distrustful human.

But even more, I want to tell you to shoot yourself and put the rest of us out of our misery.

Problem Lady

9

WHAT ARE BOUNDARY ISSUES?

BOUNDARY ISSUES, BESIDES BEING THE HOT NEW psychological malady, really exist. A person with boundary issues cannot tell where she stops and another person begins. This makes it hard to discern the difference between appropriate interactive behavior and a fucking nut haranguing you unto death. Instead of shouting when someone hurts her, a person with bad boundaries wonders what she's doing wrong and apologizes.

Having boundary issues severely hampers one's ability to have healthy relationships, but they are excellent for causing gargantuan panic attacks.

Do you have boundary issues?

Do you ever look at someone walking down the street, perhaps a woman wearing unfortunate white stretch leggings, and then get utterly depressed? Do you wonder if maybe someday, against your will, you'll turn into that woman?

Have you ever been stuck in a room with an insane person and soon become convinced you are also insane?

When couples bicker in front of you, do you want to crawl under a table?

Are you afraid of confrontation?

Are you *really* afraid of confrontation?

Are you pathologically afraid of confrontation?

Do you think that if you confront anyone about anything, even leaving a wet sock on the dining room table, they will turn on you and beat you to a lifeless shred?

When asking for something you need, even for the cabdriver to drop you on the left side, far corner, does your voice become thick with stuttering and apologies?

If you answered yes to any of the above, you are plagued.

Where do boundary issues come from?

It's all about emotional trespassing.

Did your parents ever search your room when you weren't around? Did they ever read your letters? Did your aunt ever call you a spawn of Satan and no one came to your defense? Did your father ever decide it was your fault his life sucked? Did your mother ever put you on a diet because *she* was afraid of getting fat? Were you made to feel like a loathsome excrescence, and also unattractive?

All God's creatures have rights, but until very recently parents thought of children as small lisping representations of themselves, or worse. If their children were sloppy or sad or bookish or neurotic, parents took it personally. The idea that children have the right to their own moods and thoughts and bodies and souls is extremely modern. And many immature maniacs become parents, and they fuck you up, your mom and dad.

So exactly how do boundary issues affect my relationships?

If you have boundary issues, you will not know how to choose your friends. You may choose people with nastiness issues, cruelty issues, creepy-crawly issues. People who ask you what could have possessed you to buy those shoes.

And God forbid you should just say, "Shove it up your ass." No. You will pause and think about everything you've ever said to this person, and everything this person ever said to you. You will pry through your memory to see if maybe there's a good reason that this blot would insult your shoes. And then you will decide it's better to say nothing just in case, and then you will get really depressed and eat a quart of ice cream.

No, no! Excuse me, but when I say "my relationships," I mean my sex life.

Oh, ok. Here's the boundary-challenged relationship paradigm:

1. Meet someone, become consumed with attraction and lust.
2. Have sex. Walk around in a happy daze.

3. Spend the weekend together. Fuck like bunnies.
4. Spend Monday and Tuesday nights together. Fuck like bunnies.
5. Spend Wednesday together. Feel nauseous and strange.
6. Spend Thursday together. Ready to scream with craving for solitude. Say nothing, due to intense fear. Fear of what? Abandonment, maybe! Yelling, maybe! Petulance, perhaps!
7. Practice saying, "Maybe we should take a night or two off," in front of bathroom mirror.
8. Lover sashays into bathroom. Clears throat. Says, "Er, um, ah, would it be okay if we took a couple of nights off?"
9. Go insane!
10. Get really insecure!
11. Decide lover hates you!
12. Burst into hot self-pitying tears!
13. Pick a big fight!
14. Endure three days of intense paranoia.
15. Rinse and repeat.

Again and again, someone will be madly offended by the solitude need. I would spend too much time with someone, be afraid to say anything or God forbid ask for anything, then get suffocated and become claustrophobic because I was afraid to say anything or ask for anything. Then I'd want to end the relationship. As soon as I thought that, the pendulum would swing. I would start madly projecting and be panicked that it was all over, the guy didn't like me, and I would become this horrible wimp, always in his face. It was that most awful of ironies: The more I needed to be alone, the more needy I would act, and many a time the guy would indeed stop liking me.

Although some of those suckers stuck around. Then I really hated them. They made me sick with all their smothering acceptance of me and my neediness. Those are the guys I made into mincemeat before I left. If you want to cure boundary issues, you must learn to speak out, loud and proud. Practice now. Say, "Fred, I adore you but I need some time alone. Just to be by myself."

Then mop your sweat. It'll be easier next time.

10

LISTENING TO PEANUT M&M'S

I AM IN MIDCATASTROPHE. TWO KING-SIZED BAGS OF M&M's, eaten today after 4:00 P.M. One more bag right here in bed with me, along with a stray bag of Hershey's beautiful little pastel Easter Eggs. Even though I am nauseous now, I will eat that final bag before sleeping, quite probably the Hershey's too. He's in the other room, mad at me. I have done something awful but I don't know what. I keep doing awful things. He got really hurt. I'm nervous. I want to say the right thing. He's drinking wine.

Not me. I'm eating. I feel better, I think.

I have been married for eight whole months. It is March 1997.

I shouldn't have bought them. Those egg-shaped things with the sugar crust, then chocolate, then a peanut usually inside. They melt, I believe, in your mouth, not your hand. A week ago I bought one bag. Just one. Not king-sized or anything rash. Then I bought two.

You know, he's starting to really yell. And use the word "unforgivable." Plus biblical words. Plus sarcasm. I'm nervous. I feel the way I've felt before but I can't remember when. He is so mad at me, how can I convince him I love him, there's no reason to be in a fury?

Midnight. I finished it all. He's sleeping loudly and snortily on the couch. Visions of M&M's dance in my head. It would be so easy. Just get out of bed, get dressed, find car keys, put on shoes, find purse, get in car, drive to 7-Eleven, buy a small bag. Yes! No! A big bag, because what if a small bag were not big enough? He doesn't want me to eat candy. There's a reason, I can't remember right now. I'm in bed, paralytic with indecision. I consider calling a friend since I recklessly go through life without an M&M sponsor. No, I don't need to! I can kick this thing! I can tiptoe into the kitchen and smear fat-free bagels with fat-free cream cheese and all-fruit-no-sugar preserves and be just fine.

But that sugary crust keeps appearing in my fantasies. How I would warm a handful of M&M's on my tummy, then slowly break each one open with my teeth, suck out the melting chocolate, let my tongue play lightly with the shards of sugar coating, then slam that peanut against my molars.

This is not normal food, even normal junk food. People who hate ice cream, who can easily bypass homemade children's birthday party chocolate cake or even crème brûlée, will screech to a slavering helpless halt for peanut M&M's. It is the eggness of them. A shell, chocolate placenta, proteiny peanut baby. Life shape, birth shape, cell shape, protoplasmic-ooze shape.

"Eat me, don't worry about him! Eat me, I will comfort and nourish you and never betray you, I am always here, always the same, count on me, use me, I love you."

I listen to the M&M siren call wafting from the 7-Eleven through the dark streets empty but for darting cats and cooling cars. I eat another bagel, etc. At 2:00 A.M., I am still obsessing. Four A.M., I can make it until tomorrow.

Six A.M. I wake up. He's still snoring. His lips are stained purple. I put on my raincoat over my nightie and go to the 7-Eleven, where I buy only two regular-sized bags.

Four hundred eighty calories altogether. I promise a big time on the treadmill tomorrow, I promise this is the last time I will eat M&M's until my birthday and probably not even then. Although why not get fat(ter) anyway? What's wrong with a nice cushion, a womanly heft, what's wrong with being totally unattractive completely, goddammit? Just give up life with any men, live instead life only with dogs.

I think I might be getting just a little depressed.

11

BEWARE OF LOVE AT FIRST SIGHT

I OFTEN WONDER ABOUT "HAPPILY EVER AFTER." I think it might mean "And then they were happy until she got a restraining order." Or "And they were blissful until she was afraid to leave the house." Or possibly "Although she loved his boyish antiauthoritarianism, she eventually tired of playing the cop, unfortunately not until after he depleted her entire savings account to buy a leaky sailboat."

These days I look at movies with quite the hairy eyeball.

I once was your garden-variety yearner, munching popcorn and damp with excitement while watching, say, *Baby Boom*. "Why can't I have a veterinarian who is just like Sam Shepard fall in love with me?" I would whimper to friends, who were hopelessly wondering why they couldn't have Tom Cruise or Richard Gere.

And then it happened. I became the star of my own movie! It was Love at First Sight! He swept me off my feet! He had to marry me right away! He wouldn't take no for an answer! I waltzed around on cloud nine, hormones surging, brain addled, madly *happy.*

Cut to two years later:

It was at a screening for *Hope Floats,* when I realized movies had almost ruined my life.

It had all been so sudden. One day my beloved was the stuff dreams are made of, all witty and hilarious and loving, the next day he was angry and accusing and scary. It was so shocking, so horrible. It was also really hard to get away. Luckily I had a support team, and books. Books explaining emotional abuse.

Every single book told me to beware of:

1. A potential mate wanting to make a commitment right away, being way too invested in the relationship way too soon. In other words, Love at First Sight.
2. A man refusing to take no for an answer, who will go to any lengths, including stalking, to get what he wants. In other words, the Conquering Hero.
3. A guy with a systematic campaign to lower the self-esteem of his "beloved." Who always knows better, belittles you and your efforts, and treats you with patronizing contempt. In other words, the Noble Savage.

Who knew about this? Not me. Maybe not you. So I'm here to testify: When your life turns into a movie, RUN AWAY. It *is* too good to be true. You do *not* want to be the heroine. You want to be the Eve Arden character, the wisecracking sidekick with her sweet and devoted fella. Too many women, too many times, have been ambushed.

And why? Because of *Hope Floats.*

Harry, in *Hope Floats,* is in love not only right away, but has waited for her for decades. Then he stalks her. Then makes her feel stupid and inadequate with moronic words of wisdom. Then she tells Harry she's not ready for sex and he shushes her and grabs her and has his way.

And the happy ending is that she discovers the error of her ways! She loves him too!

To think I used to fall for this stuff. Although I always thought that the rape scene in *Gone With the Wind* was way creepy, especially when Scarlett wakes up the next morning all stretching and smiling and pink. But I always loved Clark Gable bossing around Claudette Colbert fiercely in *It Happened One Night.*

And how many movies have we seen where the girl says absolutely no, keep away from me forever, and the boy keeps calling and calling while the girl stares at her answering machine, weakening, weakening, finally capitulating and flinging herself into his arms. Even my beloved *Say Anything . . . ,* and the otherwise adorable *When Harry Met Sally,* and especially *The Graduate* feature this behavior.

Luckily, the relatively recent *Hope Floats* feels like a throwback. Romantic comedies are getting better. There's less of that insulting, belittling, big-strong-man-shows-little-lady-what's-what stuff like we saw in *Romancing the Stone, Electric Horseman, Woman of the Year, Destry Rides Again* and practically everything I fall asleep to on American Movie Classics. Instead we have *The Truth About Cats and Dogs,* where the smart girl gets the guy, and *Something About Mary,* where Mary is besieged by an entire convention of stalkers, which turns the usual movie stalking convention on its head. (God forbid the woman should be the heroic pursuer and the man the nerve-racked object of her pursuit, but that is neither here nor there.)

We must always remember that Love at First Sight is a mere plot device for the film-as-sex-act metaphor. You need conflict. You need preorgasmic tension. Nobody cares if a couple falls into each other's arms in act three if in act two all they do is sip a little coffee and take tedious strolls on the beach. Love must conquer all. The course of true love must never run smooth.

In movies we call it romance, in real life call 911.

12

THE SIXTIES, STILL A PROBLEM FOR THE CHICKS

TOO MUCH BOB DYLAN

I don't remember much about the sixties, but I do remember this: It was great fun, and full of transcendental moments of clarity, a feeling that everything was new and full of startling promise. It was a time of fabulous music, fabulous drugs, fabulous sex and yet:

It still sucked for the chicks.

One of my main memories is of sitting in a commune, wearing a Betsey Johnson cobalt blue satin minidress with batwing sleeves and glass buttons, fishnet stockings, witchy high heels and a black leather silver-studded cap while I wondered, "How come I never get to pick the record?"

The guys always picked the record. The Mothers of Invention, Vanilla Fudge, Cream and the Temptations comprised about 10 percent of the music, and, of course, 90 percent was Bob Dylan. Which is fine, since I believed I would be Mrs. Bob Dylan if ever we had met, but sometimes I didn't want to hear "Ballad of a Thin Man" for the thirteenth time in a day. Maybe I wanted to hear Janis or the Kinks or Sam Cooke. I think if I had gone up to the record player and just lah-di-fucking-dah popped on my own choice of record all the mellow groovy hippie boys would have had projectile apoplexy.

It didn't help that I lived with an entire band. Todd Rundgren was the lead guitar player. This was before his psychedelic phase, this was during his intense geeky phase. Mainly he got to decide which record to play, and it had to involve a very masturbatory guitar solo. The nonband boys were almost as bad. Even the art school boys.

And that's all I remember except, wait, one more thing:

THE PERILS OF FREE LOVE

I loved my bedroom with the muted purple haze caused by Indian bedspreads hung across the windows. Especially when I was alone, burning my Buck's County incense. Which was hardly ever, since there was a ton of boy action at the bedroom door.

It was all okay as long as I had a boyfriend. The action would stay at the door and was simply a constant barrage of questions, comments, gossip and the fervent hope that I would decide to change my bra. Nobody came in the room because my "old man" would get pissed off.

When I didn't have that real girlfriend fire for anybody, there was always someone to fend off. I swear sometimes I think the other guys sent new guys right up to my room. I would sit reading on my mattress on the floor when out of nowhere would appear Barry, or Roger, or Peter or Bobby. And maybe Bobby would say, "Wanna fuck?" because he was so fucking liberated, and I would sigh, put my head in hand and say, Nah, not in the mood and he would feel two feet tall and go. Or maybe Peter would come in and talk about jazz musicians and, you know, Trane and Bird and eventually I'd turn my face to the wall and he'd leave. Or Roger, petulant and needy, or Barry, smug and thoughtless, would say, "Whassa matter? Uptight? What are you afraid of?"

I could have said, "Let me tell you about the bald heads and the lame skinny ponytails you're going to have in thirty years, when you *still* won't be able to get laid," but who knew?

It would also have been good to mention browbeating for sex. But I didn't. I had nothing to compare to this experience. I knew nothing of women's inalienable rights to the control of and access to their own bodies. I just knew that you couldn't say, "Elliott, how *dare* you! I am not that kind of girl!" anymore. During the sixties, it was supposed to be cool to be just madly casual about sex, and I suppose it was good not to automatically be branded as a slut. Although, since these guys had generally the same upbringing as I did, it just seemed that I had one less argument to fend off men who were determined to fuck me. For me, the sixties was always a battle of wits, having these long discussions that were so boring, telling a fellow no, I was NOT uptight, I was NOT afraid, please could he just understand that I had my own reasons? But he would still press and finally, finally I would say, Look, you are an ugly, smelly motherfucker! Go brush your teeth, take a bath, buy new clothes and then maybe somewhere in the universe some girl will fuck you, but not me.

Yes, we had the Pill. But still, we did not have abortion rights! If you were pregnant, you had to get money to go to Mexico!

Another thing: During the sixties, it was proclaimed that there was no such thing as sexual jealousy. Hahahahahahahaha-hahahahahahahahahahahahahahahahahaha. Oh, also: Hahaha-hahahahahahahahahahahahahahahahahahahahahahahahahaha-hahahaha.

Ha! Ha!

Ha!

HAHA!!!

PREDATORS OR MENTORS? OR JUST THE ACID?

In the name of freedom, bad things happened. The edicts of free love with no jealousy plus the advent of LSD made it easy for sexual and emotional predators to screw us big time. Timothy Leary, Mr. Acid, lived up in Millbrook in the sixties. My semiboyfriend, who went to a high-class university, went with a bunch of pals to Millbrook to pay homage. And Timothy Leary returned the favor by giving my boyfriend STP and fucking him in the butt. I know this because my boyfriend was still high when he came home and told me about it, the expression on his face beatifically psychotic. He didn't go back to school, he became a spaced-out cook to a guru named Murray (not a Mel Brooks joke).

Lots of people who wanted to fuck other people gave them hallucinogens. Which is disgusting and wrong. There was a girl who lived in the apartment behind mine. Named Alice, nice Catholic-school girl, full of sweetness and chastity to the point where she really got on your nerves. But Alice was way more disturbing after a series of horny guys gave her a series of sugar cubes. She swore and fucked everyone. Her voice became lower and rougher. You could argue that Alice was just showing the other side of the Catholic girl coin. But I was there and I know that the acid took her personality and slowly, surely disintegrated it. Like an Oreo dipped in milk, Alice just diffused.

At one point I had a roommate I didn't like much. He was okay though, a scientist. We took acid together. While on acid—which wasn't all bad, I did after all discover the meaning of life and the fabric of God—the scientist and I decided we were in love. It was probably the insanity caused by listening to "Mr. Tambourine Man" one hundred times. And you know what? We stayed together for a year. I was miserable with him constantly lecturing me on sexual jealousy hahahahaha, which he had and I didn't. He had been a successful scientist, I had been a successful panhandler. We descended into living in a cold-water flat in a condemned house. He made drugs and I waitressed. Horrible. If we were lucky we ate one roll with cream cheese a day.

When things became really bad, he decided we should take acid together again, you know, to get back our magickal bond. It didn't work, thank the aforementioned fabric of God!!! Finally I ran away. I bought this new album called *Blonde on Blonde* and holed up in my friend Cookie's flat for a solid month, hiding from the ever more vehemently searching scientist. I played *Blonde on Blonde on Blonde* over and over and over. Cookie took me to the hippie shrink, Dr. Robert Blumberg. The man saved my life. He read me "The Love Song of J. Alfred Prufrock." He explained to me that my parents were completely insane!!! And he talked to me about acid.

"Every trip has the same effect on your brain as a childhood trauma," he said. "Just as strong, just as bad. Don't take it anymore." Acid: Not good for you. I had one trip, it felt great! Ruined me for a year.

That was the year I was most susceptible to the predators. I let too many men do too many things to me. Scary things I don't want to repeat, because still, all these hundreds of decades later, I'm so ashamed. There was the sailor who assaulted me in the movie theater while we watched *The Collector.* There was the man who told me he was going to make me a model. Fucking pedophiles. I was frozen with the fear of saying no to men who seemed older, men who seemed commanding. I couldn't speak. Guys, don't try this with me now.

Then there were the mentors who weren't criminal, but whose feet of clay could cause young fervent hippies to stumble and fall splat. I have heard that Stokely Carmichael, leader of the Black Panthers and cute enough to be every girl's wet dream, opined that the position for women in the "revolution" (hahahaha) was prone. I for one was heartbroken. Stokely, are you out there? Stokely? Are you sorry?

And, yet, it was an amazing time. Every few months a Beatles or Rolling Stones album would be released. We would love to pop on Day-Glo clothes and dance around under black light to Bothar and the Hand People music. You know? So you *should* still be pathetically jealous, you poor suckers who are all too young to remember it.

THE LATE SIXTIES, EARLY SEVENTIES

There were a couple of good things about my hometown of Philadelphia.

1. If you were a *Jules et Jim* freak, you might never meet another *Jules e. J.* freak, but if you did, she would be real. Whereas in New York City, people knew that *Jules and Jim* was "hip." François Truffaut and his *nouvelle vague* was hipper than hip. So you'd have all these pretentious twits pretending they liked *Jules et Jim* who had no fucking idea what they were talking about.
2. You'd get to meet a lot of people before they hit New York and became famous.

The seven "hippies" in Philadelphia all hung around the central-west benches of Rittenhouse Square. Anybody who came through, we met them. One day in the early spring of the mid-sixties, when I was a semistarving teenage runaway, this really sweet guy with his two front teeth missing saw me staring at a big roast beef in the window of a deli. Thus he determined that I was hungry and bought me a giant meal. I saw him again and he bought me another meal. The third time he said, "I'm playing at the Second Frett, do you know it?"

The Second Frett was the big coffeehouse in Center City, famous for folk music and French onion soup. I thought this tooth-challenged guy must be tripping. But he turned out to be Richie Havens. He never even tried to get into my pants, he was just nice!

Like Arlo Guthrie, who was around a LOT. I met him again later, when the sixties were over. "Used to be," he said, "you'd walk down the street and just *know* who had a roach in his pocket. Now everybody who looks like a freak is actually the man, and it's all ruined."

In approximately 1968 the innocence was lost and the record companies signed everybody up and hippiedom was chewed up and spat out as predigested pap in the media. I remember when I saw my first press release for a band, when the "underground" music stations became mainstream and people realized there was money in them thar kids. I remember vividly when the term "hippie" came into being, minted by *Time* magazine, and how we laughed and booed! We were co-opted! Fucking nerve!

Woodstock seemed like the death knell. It was all just too big and hairy and there was too much brown acid. "Fucking lemmings!" I yelled from the backseat of a green VW bug that held four adults and two dogs as I looked at the sea of maniacs determined to storm the Woodstock stage. I was three months pregnant, and in no mood. That night we slept in the field of a nearby farm, sure that our heads were going to be crushed like melons by a tractor. We felt defeated.

But we weren't. Haha. Society tried to absorb and change us, and we tried to absorb and change society. Nobody lost, nobody won, we just all got corrupted. We sure changed things though! We gave the world a blow job–loving president and "visualize whirled peas" bumper stickers.

But it all would have died a placid death without feminism.

Because the pendulum swings. We all got really scared by that brown acid. We all suddenly wanted to go straight and settle down in the most tedious way.

These were the robot years.

During my childhood seeds were planted. Talking seeds. They said, "You will get married. You will have children. You will be a good housewife. You will make the beds with hospital corners. You will listen to your man, who is the boss. It is all about your carpets and your looks. Wear a white glove to check for dust."

But I ran away, far away and kept going until one day in 1968 I had gone too far, swung around the Horn and started on my way back. I became the Frankenstein Monster waltzing around chanting Must Get Married. Must Settle Down. Must Get Married. Where Is Husband?

Husband-type, Steve, was found. Nice friendly hippie man with a good, smart lovable family. Pregnancy was achieved. A proposal was made on bended knee. Pregnancy failed. Got married anyway. Got a cream-colored polyester satin dress at Macy's for the wedding. It wasn't even shoplifted. We cried and cried during the wedding ceremony, allegedly with happiness, but I think we knew we were kissing our hippie days good-bye, entering into the conventional lives promulgated by our conventional families. WAH!

Pregnancy was achieved again, we went to aforementioned

Woodstock, didn't care about the Who or Abbie Hoffman or anybody. Cared about pregnancy. Baby was born on April 27, 1970. Could anybody have known that he would get married on *I Got Married During Spring Break,* in his bathing suit, on MTV, in Vegas? No.

IV

ALPHA BITCH SOUP

13

WOMEN'S INTUITION?

DO WOMEN HAVE A SPECIAL LOCUS IN THE BRAIN, possibly a node or even a nodule, that gives them a greater power than men to see the concealed, hear the mute, grasp the unfathomable? Is there really such a thing as women's intuition?

No.

Thank you and good night.

You know the kind of day when you can't decide whether to shoot yourself or have a pedicure? When your everyday concerns fade into the background and your actual elemental self is

Originally appeared in *Playboy* magazine.

so exposed and vulnerable and you know that everything you do is critical to the entire future of your sanity? When a wisp of a thread dangling from a shirt cuff stands out in stark relief and has insanely crucial ramifications but you don't know what they are so you compulsively play computer solitaire?

That's intuition knocking at the door, demanding to be let in with some kind of new fresh hell of an insight. Men have it, just not as often as women. Because intuition is not extrasensory, genetic or magical. Intuition is the product of adaptive behavior. And in this society, women have had to adapt more than men. Oh, yes they do.

Look, please, at traditional childhood conditioning. Say we're at any playground. Little Freddie, a hothead, smacks another boy with his Frisbee. Freddie's mom gets annoyed and tells Freddie to stop that right now. The other parents shrug with "Whattayagonnado, you don't want no sissy" expressions. Freddie's mom smiles ruefully and goes back to her mystery novel.

Later on, little Emily smashes another kid in the knee with her shovel. Emily's mom grabs her and hisses out a big lecture, the gist being "Little girls don't behave that way." The other parents look away, embarrassed at the spectacle of the pint-sized hoyden. When Emily and Mom leave, the term "bad seed" hangs in the air.

Little Freddie, censured for his behavior, has a still-intact sense of self. But little Emily is not criticized for her behavior but for who she *is.*

This is a big deal.

Emily (I'm becoming attached to my creation) is systematically taught to deny the aggressive, greedy part of herself. It doesn't matter if she just hates the sight of some booger-head kid and wants to show him who's boss or if some stupid bully steals her crayons. Tough shit, Emily. Little girls don't hit and punch. Little girls are made of sweetness and spice and candied violets and puppy breath. No bone, muscle or grit. Tell your mommy, your daddy, or your big brother. They'll take care of you.

Thus does a girl learn passivity and helplessness. (Before you start sending me angry e-mail, I know little Em is a stereotype cooked up by my brain. Mileage varies in actual lives. Yet the vast majority of children were in fact raised with these notions.) If the girl is taught never to be direct, the woman will be intuitive. She is intuitive so she can learn to manipulate people.

What the hell else is she supposed to do, cross her fingers and pray that jobs, mates, happiness fall into her lap? If you've been brainwashed by your parents and your culture to never show angry aggression and to never simply go out and take what you want, you have to be sneaky. You play people. You figure out how to get them to do what you want without asking them.

Which means you get really, really good at picking up the teeniest clues, the subtlest of innuendos. A slightly averted glance or a twitching finger can mean volumes. After years of practice, you don't even have to think, you just know all kinds of stuff about that guy over in the corner at the cocktail party.

And the more repressive and narrow the upbringing, the more a woman or a man is equipped with mind-reading capabilities. Psychics, I'm guessing, were brought up entirely in sealed cardboard boxes. And plenty of us had appalling childhood incidents that jump-started the intuitive process.

Say, for example, you're me. You go to some kind of allegedly *enlightened* summer camp where nobody's supposed to have any hang-ups and the counselors—blonde Aryan teenagers—force you to undress in front of everybody and ridicule and abuse you if you try to hide or cry or do anything besides what they tell you, and you do not fight back. The fucking sadistic bastards. I hope they're living lives of desperate misery somewhere. Oh, sorry. But you see what I'm saying.

And men who've had lousy childhoods are the most intuitive bastards I know, even more than women, because men do not, as a rule, share and therefore assuage bad feelings.

Even average men have fleeting intuitions. They call these "gut feelings." These gut feelings are often ignored, because they don't jibe with surface realities. Your accountant suddenly has a shifty vibe, you figure you're just paranoid: Mavis is a good gal, she's been doing your taxes for years! But follow that paranoia, see where it leads. Maybe Mavis is just having troubles at home, but maybe she is building up a nice bank account in the Cayman Islands.

Feelings and hunches are always in some way valid. Pay attention. Probe the queasy spot in your psyche, it's not just a random tic, it's real information. The more you dig, the more truth will come to the surface.

It may be ugly, it may crash your system for a while, but the truth is a good thing to know, even if the truth is that your mate is unfaithful, or your boss is a liar, or you were humiliated and abused as a child.

The truth will set you free. Lah-di-fucking-dah.

14

MY LIFE AS A MAN

I WENT SHOPPING TODAY. IT WAS HEAVEN. SUCH A relief, going into a giant department store, combing through tights, feeling the differing textures of scarves between my fingertips, trying on jackets and dresses slowly and deliberately, doing my world-famous Marilyn-Monroe-on-acid poses in front of the mirror.

Way more fun than being on testosterone.

I just don't see how men do it, having such a hormone pumping through their bodies day and especially night. How

Originally appeared in *Playboy* magazine.

do guys ever *think?* Or choose, or ponder, or find underwear?

Why, only yesterday afternoon, I almost committed girl felony. I was at my close friend Lucy's for tea and ended up next to her husband Paul on their sofa. It is a small sofa. I had always theoretically known that Paul is an attractive fellow—beautiful greeny-blue eyes, thick brown hair shot with red and gold, tall, muscular, oh my God. Paul sat inches from me. He was watching football. It took all my strength to keep my hand from running rampant over his thigh. Fantastically detailed sexual fantasies leapt from my brain straight to my groin. I believe I began panting.

By now I have every confidence that you are asking yourself, "What the fuck?"

I'm glad you asked. I met a couple of fabulous lesbians from Australia. They said testosterone made you all horny and aggressive and, well, manly. I was riveted. Who knew that people could just *take* testosterone? Naturally I wanted some immediately. I could find out what makes guys guys! Have the kind of brain that can actually understand what a carburetor is! Differentiate my right brain from my left! Be the sort of person who says he's going to call and then doesn't!

My doctor said that a day or two of wearing a testosterone patch would not cause me to grow a beard or anything. He gave me a prescription for testosterone patches! Yes!

The pharmacist looked at me kind of funny. I paid her, and took the patches home, went into the bathroom, applied them to my skin and heated them up with a hair dryer as directed, and waited.

The stuff hit me while I was sitting at the computer. Suddenly the screen was all bright and the rest of the room looked much darker. I shook my head, confused. Shook it again. Everything still looked weird. I wondered if I was having a sudden brain tumor. Wherever I looked, things were either bright, or dark. No modulation, high contrast, very weird.

Then the guys came over to watch football. Forced me to drink beer, eat those horrible orange corn chips. The beer bored me, but the football game was entirely interesting. My gut twitched sideways when the quarterback was sacked. *My* quarterback. He was my guy, part of my gang, nobody better fuck with him. And when *my* team won, I was unrecognizable to myself. Normally when they show the losing team on TV I worry about them. I want them to feel better. Not now. Now I wanted them annihilated, even more.

We went out to some nightclub to see if I suddenly wanted to pick up broads. I didn't. All my mounting lust was directed toward men.

I was quite fabulous at that bar. Everything I said was smart, witty, important, cogent. I had many fascinating stories to tell, and I just knew everyone was interested, that my perceptions were more fascinating than anyone else's. In some deep cavity of my brain I wondered if this was simply the testosterone, but it couldn't be. I was just too brilliant is all.

I drove home and wanted anyone who cut me off on the freeways immediately dead. I reveled in the power of my truck. I was bigger and faster than anyone.

I got home and phoned my son.

"Call me Dad," I said.

"Get a life," he said.

The next morning I was really surly. Nobody could do anything right. The cellular phone company tried to fuck with me. They didn't get away with it. I wasn't in the mood to cuddle the dogs. I was tired of my new weird eyesight, bored with everyone phoning and asking if I had suddenly got the hots for girls. Everything was pissing me off.

And my lust was growing. Usually I feel lust when there is reason to feel lust. During sex. Watching Dennis Quaid in *The Big Easy.* Eating large carrots. But now my lust was a constant, just sitting there in my body, waiting for something to attach it to. The guy doing the weather on TV looked great. The UPS man, a weedy little weirdo, took on an interesting vibe. And then Paul, my friend's husband, put me over the top.

I tore myself away from Paul. Drove home all sweaty and nauseous. Knocked over a couple of my neighbors' trash cans as I swung my truck into the driveway. Ran into the house, sat down on the floor as a wave of dizziness careened through my head.

Horrible stuff, this stuff! Not funny anymore. No wonder teenaged boys go goofy and violent, with this pumping drive suddenly coming upon them. This is stuff that needs major micromanagement. Something that swings your mind around whether you want it to or not. All women should try it for a day to see what men deal with. All men should try estrogen once or twice, maybe when they have to decorate their houses.

I pulled up my skirt, ready to rip off those pesky patches.

(Maybe I shouldn't have used three when I was told to use one. I was never any good at following drug directions.)

But I stopped. I had one more thing to do. I went into the bedroom and masturbated. A harsh, really short orgasm. Like ten seconds instead of a minute or so.

Ten seconds. What's the point?

15

MEN: THE DEFAULT SEX

WHAT'S SO FUNNY ABOUT A MAN IN A DRESS?

I saw that genius Steven Wright on a *Letterman* rerun the other night. He said he was having this chronic nightmare. He brought a clip. (How genius is that?)

In the clip he was sitting and talking to Dave wearing a little flowered librarian dress, carrying a prim purse, and wearing sensible heels. Just talking normally.

Why, I need to know, did I just about die laughing?

I remember the first time I saw a woman in a man's suit. 1968, Bloomingdale's. The suit spoke to me. "What are *you* looking at?" it snarled. It was unbelievably cool. Still is. Periodically the fashion magazines decree a menswear-for-women frenzy; pinstripes make a big statement in fall's fashion pages every other year. But a woman in men's clothing is always considered chic (unless she's sporting an aqua polyester leisure suit, which will not be cool until next year). In movies, our heroine is a tomboy and always sleeps in giant football jerseys. And too damn many of us refuse to be without our Calvins.

A woman in men's clothes is very normal. A woman in extreme men's clothes may mean she's a big ole lesbian but this is not innately hilarious.

Yet men's magazines do not feature crinolines. A man in an evening gown is a man who is a drag queen. Your basic male breeder would rather have shingles than wear a dress. On a TV sitcom, it's a surefire laugh if our hero gets caught in a marabou-encrusted negligee. Is there something innately ridiculous about femininity? Is it simply that penises and sequins just don't match? Do big biceps look out of place with lace?

I trotted out some theories about this at a dinner party. Unfortunately, it was a dinner party full of Texans. They hooted and hollered and pretended to believe that I'd proposed that in a Utopian feminist society, all men would be forced into pouf skirts.

"Are women in men's clothing just aping the oppressor and it is therefore okay?" I asked. "Is it as simple as the fact that in our society men are the default sex and wearing the outfits of the underclass occasions ridicule?"

"You've always wanted to see me go strapless," said James, a big man with a beard who used to be my boyfriend.

"Is it homosexual panic?" I asked. "And if it is, isn't that a subset of the above? Being a gay woman does not occasion ridicule, being a gay man too often does. Would this be because there is much belief in the superiority of men?"

"I like my men rugged," said Lynn Ann, James's wife.

"Maybe it's the frontier ethic that makes it all so distasteful to you," I hypothesized. "You know, that be-a-man, shoot-Old-Yeller-but-don't-cry kind of stuff? The heavy mantle of masculinity. You all want to be cowboys. Even if you were from Connecticut, you still wanna herd them dogies."

The guys just kept teasing me about how they wanted to wear peplums, and silk-satin gowns cut on the bias, and Manolo Blahnik heels. I wondered at their excellent fashion vocabulary.

I think I'm right about this being a masculine world, still! Men: the default sex.

Yet things are inching toward change. Young trendy men of all persuasions wear nail polish and earrings on *both* ears. Who can forget Kurt Cobain in his lipstick and dresses? Penn Jillette, the large macho magician, enjoys a bubble bath. Dennis Rodman, the best rebounder in history and still extremely sexy, fancies himself in a wedding dress.

A week after the dinner with the Texans I had a birthday party at my house. Big Boy made a big entrance—in a lovely floral muumuu, hat, and pearls.

I fell on the floor, pissing myself laughing.

16

BITCH! BITCH! BITCH?

SO I'M ONLINE THE OTHER DAY, AND MY FRIEND IN Florida tells me this heartwarming story about how she went to a restaurant to apply for a hostess job. About twenty women were ahead of her, all of them simpering. The manager interviewing them was enjoying his power just a little too much: His face glistened with condescension. The applicants responded with placating platitudes and submissive postures, but when the manager got to my pal she said, "I'll be the best worker you ever had, but don't even *try* to fuck with me."

Originally appeared in *Playboy* magazine.

The guy hired her on the spot.

"Men do *love* a bitch," she said.

They do, I thought. I remembered specific times when I was in work mode, trying to get a story done, and if any man got in my way I bulldozed right over him. After which the guy started wagging his tail and asking for my phone number. I hardly noticed or cared, because in work mode I am implacable. In work mode I am a bitch.

Whereas in dating mode there was a time when I was perhaps a bit soft. Somewhat timid. Okay! Yes! When dating I have been a craven, yellow-bellied, spineless pantywaist! Boy, have boys walked all over me.

When I was interested in someone, fear would settle over me like a cloak. A guy would call, casually invite me over. Did I say, "Sorry, I'm busy, give me a little more notice next time"? Hah.

"I'll be right there," I'd say, and I'd rush madly into and out of the shower, slather on makeup, throw on clothes, spray a cloud of perfume and walk through it and sprint out the door. Then I'd run back in the door and into the bathroom and have fear diarrhea, which I'm sure nobody has but me.

A couple of years ago a man I was really crazy about did one of those special male things of which I had become so fond. I'll spare you the play-by-play. Suffice to say that after a couple of months of mild fooling around and major chat fests, I got the phone call: "I really like you, but I'm just seeing too many other women."

Well. Floods of tears. The ritualistic calling of all friends and recounting every moment of the phone call. Emergency shrink session. Hiding under the bed and muttering.

And then I crossed a crucial line. After one million years of dating, I had finally had enough. A small stubborn voice buried within the very essence of my soul said, "Fuck this. I am fucking not taking any more fucking shit."

And reader, just like that, I became a bitch. A holy terror on dates. And, holy shit, the men began to flock. At first I thought it was because I had given up and didn't care. But soon I knew the obvious answer: Men go for bitches—women who spare no feelings, who assume no submissive postures, who will be aggressive and suffer no fools.

But why? Naturally I went to the Well. The Well is an online bulletin board full of smart-asses; it's like a small town where we all know each other's business, who each other is fucking, what each other needs. Where we advise, tease, meddle and construct secret private conferences to talk about everybody beyond their backs. Well people are full of opinions and everybody was glad to enlighten me.

"A bitch reminds us of Mom," wrote (mz).

"More like, reminds us of someone with the guts to take Mom on. Such women are a lot easier to deal with," wrote (josh). "They'll tell us just where we stand (no mind-reading necessary); we don't have to walk on eggshells lest some rule we might not have known about gets violated. The Bitch is as likely to be the protector as we are; the Bitch is also as likely to be a provider as we are; one rarely fears that the Bitch cannot make it on her own."

"So are we saying it's about—dare I say it?—boundaries?" I wrote back. "If someone is too sweetie-nice, does this mean you'll be the center of her universe, which is not madly attractive?"

"You're on to something there," wrote (grifter). "I've got enough problems living my own life that I don't much relish somebody else living hers through me."

"I like the notion that I won't have to handle or be in charge of everything," wrote (jrc). "Because then if I fuck up, it's okay, I've got some kind of backup. Also if I wanna whine or moan, there won't be some delicate flower dissolving in tears. Plus, I love the lace-up boots."

"There are times I've been an idiot," wrote (ivanski). "And I *know* so; if she calls me on it, I'm more comfortable owning up to stupidity than pretending I'm fucking perfect."

One of the many boyfriends I acquired after achieving bitchitude threatened suicide when I tried to break up with him. What a creepy, off-putting ploy. Nobody (of either sex) wants to feel she has so much power in a relationship that she can destroy her insignificant other. If you can't live without me, die already.

This boyfriend's needy antics put me into the place of all those boys for whom I wasted all those years trying to impersonate a doormat. I felt smothered, trapped. I wanted to sprint in the opposite direction.

But, who knows, maybe that's just me.

"It's not just you," wrote everybody.

17

MOTHERING MADE EASY

WELL, PREGNANCY IS GOOD. YOU'VE GOT SOMETHING swimming inside you, getting bigger and bigger. Turns you all inner-directed. It's all about you and your needs, and everybody better hop to it and bring you French fries and mangoes. Stat!

Too bad nobody thought to say to you, "Go out to dinner every night, then go to the movies, because you never will again. And, by the way, you won't be sleeping, ha ha ha. Also, you'll become incredibly boring."

So you have your baby, and you remember every ounce of the pain, and you don't sleep, and you get postpartum depression, which is a big black mood cloud that lasts for months. And your baby is colicky, so you spend every minute in bed eating cookies, drinking Guinness Stout for the B vitamins and suckling baby—except when baby is extra colicky and you have to take her out to the car and drive her around to get her to sleep.

You are now officially incredibly boring. You know how madly boring you are, but you cannot help yourself. You will try to buttonhole strangers to discuss the merits of various breast pumps; they will back away nervously.

Everyone told you but you never understood about the searing and consuming and mind-altering love. Everybody else's baby: Boring. Your baby: Every molecule of every toenail is sacred. This response happens because that's the way you are made. Everything in your brain and body is fashioned for this childbirth, this child-rearing. It goes way deeper than your conscious mind; baby love informs your DNA. The smell, touch, sound of your baby leaves you breathless and gasping from the torrents of perfect and terrible love.

And there's also wild anger and mind-numbing monotony and plain old motherly exasperation and then, naturally, the guilt. No bad feelings! Bad feelings are bad! You must be the perfect mother all the time, every minute of every day, or else your child will grow up to say, "Please, God, don't let me turn into my mother."

Oh, there are those petty competitions with other mothers to have the child who lifts her head first, who rolls over the earliest, who sits up before six months, who walks at eight months, who reads entire sentences at age three. Your child, do or die!

Does anyone look at your child with anything other than admiration and awe? If so, that person must be deleted immediately from your PalmPilot.

Your days go by as you make little and then bigger breakfasts, and you wash infinitesimal shirts and nightgowns, then bigger, striped pullovers that have watercolor stains on the sleeves. You learn to make big rules. No going even near the street. No going on the roof. No cookies before lunch. No French-kissing the cat. No, you may not turn over that bowl of potato chips, no matter how hilarious it seems.

You think, "This will go on forever. I will never get a minute's peace. I will always be finding melted crayons in the dryer." Then you think, "What if this doesn't go on forever? OH NO! My child will never grow up and leave home. Never. Other children do, perhaps, but NOT MINE. I will not have it!" You look at your child narrowly. Is she growing again? Is she now up to your waist, now up to your armpits, now up to your chin?

What exactly is the deal with this? You tailor your goddamn life around this goddamn kid, goddammit, and now this kid is growing up, and now she is going to the prom! Now she's talking college! But she will of course go to college nearby, she will of course live at home. Forever. Or else.

Else happens. Distant colleges tempt your faithless child. You can't stand it. No, you really cannot. You will be bereft, you will be too lonely to live, you will lose your sense of purpose and self. Nobody should expect this of a saint, let alone of you.

She goes. She's off. She hates it, and she calls you all the time. She loves it, and you never hear from her. She changes majors. She talks of strangers. She comes home for weekends. She graduates. She goes to work. She has a life. It all happens, just the way it's supposed to. And you?

You get a dog. Maybe four.

18

HARDWIRED

FIRST OF ALL CAN WE JUST LOAD A SPACESHIP FULL OF those "scientists" who use "Darwinian" theory to further their own wet dreams? These inane studies that show us that men would rather fuck a young wide-hipped girl with big eyes whose name is Kate Moss? That self-serving research by womanizing twits to help other womanizing twits fuck around on their wives and girlfriends?

We do not trust scientific fact that is too convenient or too incredibly stupid. Perhaps it was true once that men were primarily attracted to youth (I doubt it, since men as we know are attracted to anything that moves and is slippery. But say it was true). That was then, when the species was interested in furthering itself, when the entire earth wasn't full of burping snorting farting humans polluting and co-opting and generally making a huge nuisance of themselves. Now the human species is being way more circumspect and selecting for oh, I'm guessing brains, money, infertility, and a good grasp of Unix.

While it is true that our bodies are annoyingly Stone Age in many respects—they are still *shocked* that we're not walking on all fours, ergo, lower back pain—our brains are infinitely myriad in their adaptabilities. So, yes, while part of my brain responds droolingly to a nice bulging biceps, more of it goes goopy mad loony for a man conversant in all aspects of the oeuvre of P. G. Wodehouse. The BF, when he wants to get laid, just opens *The Code of the Woosters* at any random page and reads aloud, and I immediately go all slippery and demand to be spanked and tied up at least. And what do you have to say to that, contributors to the *Science Times*?

Nonetheless, we are all totally animals. Animals with a surface layer of consciousness that tells us all sorts of shit about logic and choice and right and wrong and reality and fantasy, which is all big ole lies and rationalizations. Underneath this consciousness shell, this weird adaptation that makes us think we are somehow separate from the chimps and rhinos and spiders, is a teeming morass of hot incessant instinctive behaviors and drives.

For example:

Jealousy.

Repeat after me: A jealous rage is not learned behavior. A jealous rage is not negotiable. A jealous rage comes cascading to our brains from deep within the core of our beings.

Look at dogs, whose jealousy is so cute when they push in front of each other to get a coveted pat on the head, whose jealousy is less cute when two bitches fight to the death for supremacy. Look at tomcats who kill kittens. Look at chimps. Look at elephants.

Jealousy, far from being an abnormality, is in fact a primary evolutionary drive. Just like sex. Just like eating French fries. If your mate tells you s/he isn't jealous, you can be sure that means one of two things:

S/he is a great big liar.

S/he doesn't care whether you live or die.

So watch it.

Other hardwired, innate behaviors:

1. The fear of crossing large bodies of water. For example, I live in Oakland. No one will come and visit me from San Francisco, nor will I undertake the entire twelve minutes of driving even to ride on one of San Francisco's world-famous streetcars, or sample some lovely Rice-A-Roni.
2. The need to be home by dark. I don't know about you, maybe you're way too evolved to feel a horrid anxiety when in a strange place.
3. Getting sleepy and sedentary in the rain. You *want* to go out to that movie, you *want* to get out of bed, but . . . zzzzzzzzzzzzzzzzzzzzzzzzzzzzzz.
4. Selective eye contact. You gonna lock eyes with that homunculus strolling down the street toting an automatic submachine gun? Whereas if you see an attractive human at a cocktail party, if you don't make eye contact before looking away coquettishly, how are you ever going to get laid?

5. Snarling and spitting: Go ahead, get really furiously, lividly angry. See what happens.
6. Making up any kind of lame shit you can think of to excuse your insane sexual behavior, like, for instance, Woody Allen saying, "The heart wants what it wants," or the typical white boy science writer who posits that it is evolutionarily sound for men to screw small-waisted, large-hipped teenagers who have wide-set symmetrical eyes, even when they are married grandfathers.
7. Being convinced that you are always, always right.

19

PROBLEM LADY

Dear Problem Lady:

Is the backlash over? Can we relax for a second?

Women are holding some of the highest jobs in the land, and my boyfriend is picking up wet towels.

Even the guys where I work, a porcine bunch, have been sheepishly conciliatory lately.

Sometimes I think women are now on a straight, sure road to success. But then as soon as I think that, I get a tiny black feeling in the pit of my stomach.

Lola

Dear Lola:

Okay, first we have to define success. There are some, like Naomi (don't hate me because I'm beautiful) Wolf, who tend to define success in traditional testosterone terms: conquering, winning, beating the system at its own game, cutting off other guys' heads, etc.

It is quite possible that women could enter this fray and become more and more successful, but we would be shooting our species in the foot. Because testosterone tactics are outmoded, passé, over. Even men think so. Some men. Anyway, a few.

These seven men have realized that while looting and pillaging and hostile takeovers were okay for the Stone Age, our world is now in a precarious position, and that the very characteristics that make our species strong contain their own seeds of destruction, which are now bearing fruit (whew!).

Everything in the world is now trapped, tamed, conquered, screwed. There's no more land to forage, no more alleged savages to toast, and now we must protect all wild animals from *us*.

Now with the new millennium, the testosterone era wanes. We're evolving slowly but slowly away from the patriarchy to who the hell knows what.

Wait, where was I?

Oh yeah. The backlash is still with us, but also evolving. Once women just wanted to enter men's world, now they want to redefine it.

And although individual enlightened men may be willing to relinquish power, those entrenched in the power structure are still fighting tooth and testes. Still holding up straw feminists like Naomi Wolf to divert us. Still looking for any chink in women's collective self-worth in order to undermine. Still throwing degrading and objectifying images of women at us from every TV and movie screen at their disposal.

Those men, and the even more dangerous women who identify with them, know they are becoming dinosaurs. They're getting greedy and creepy and desperate. Their latest is making every teenager wanting to be too skinny to live.

It's never time to relax vigilance.

Problem Lady

* * *

Dear Problem Lady:

My son and my husband are at it again. I'm hiding in the bedroom wearing earplugs, but their yelling is still splitting my head apart.

How did this happen? They used to play basketball, baseball and ride bikes together. They used to gang up on me. My husband glowed when he looked at the kid, the kid thought the sun shone out of my husband's butt.

Now, everything and anything can trigger a huge explosion. My husband accidentally stepped on my son's shoelaces, sent the guy sprawling. Which is why I'm in the bedroom plugging my ears.

Neither of them makes any sense, both of them have turned into monsters, I'm going crazy.

And they look exactly alike. A sixteen-year-old kid and a forty-eight-year-old man with the same face. Now always contorted. They won't go to counseling.

Maggie

Dear Maggie:

Pity the parent of the same-sex child. A father is his son's role model, his idol, his god, until the hormones start rearing up and the kid realizes he has to separate from his hero. Separating, always painful, is usually accomplished by rebellious, recalcitrant, really irritating behavior.

And meanwhile Dad is hitting midlife crisis time, when he's decided his looks are starting to go and he's entreating the gods to let his dick keep working for a few more years. So of course he's just thrilled to look at his sweet little boy turning all virile and horny and hairy.

They'll get over it. They always do.

Problem Lady

* * *

Dear Problem Lady:

My dad went crazy when I said I was planning to change my name.

"The last of the Buckenlatkas and my son decides it's not good enough for him?" Dad screamed and threw a glass at me.

Then he called my Aunt Estelle, who called all the cousins, and now the whole family is up in arms. Every day I have to fend off another uncle.

I've been a good son—sober, responsible, not always respectable but close. I'm even in med school, just like he wanted. I just can't stand being Phil Buckenlatka one more second.

Don't you think I have the right to do this? Is it really the end of the world?

Phil

Dear Phil:

Have you covered your body with X-rated tattoos? Taken every drug you can find? Robbed banks or molested chickens? Probably not. For this, Dad should be proud.

Here's what you do. Tell him, "Dad, I'm going to quit school. I am a heroin addict."

When he goes insane, say, "Just kidding. I would never do anything so totally crazy. I'm just going to change my name. Wanna make something of it?"

He won't.

Problem Lady

* * *

Dear Problem Lady:

My daughter hates her job and wants to come home. Karen is twenty-four and graduated college two years ago. My husband is thrilled. Right now he's clipping the hedges, humming. He never clips the hedges.

I am not so thrilled. Much as I love her. And I know what you're thinking, so just cut it out right now. You're thinking, "Aha! Tired, fading mother feels competitive toward daughter! Mother with gray all over her head which she tries hopelessly to hide but after two days the goddamned gray starts poking out at the temples doesn't want to be confronted on a daily basis with nubile young woman! Mother with skin like a cornhusk, mother whose butt resembles the moon, mother who can never again even pretend to wear a miniskirt, does not need these flaws underlined and highlighted by some little pisher old enough to be her daughter!"

Just shut up! That's not it at all. And if you don't believe me, fuck you.

The thing is, it's not like she's starving. It's not like she's wasting away in some Turkish prison somewhere. She has an apartment and friends and a car. She just happens to have one of those shitty jobs where her boss is this low-level management flunky with no power except over one measly person, so Boss-woman makes Karen's life hell.

I know the feeling, both my husband and I have had such shitty jobs. Karen doesn't believe this, since now we are well-known musicians and make money.

"Why should she be tortured just because we were?" my husband says. "Let her come home until she finds something right for her!"

"You just want to have your little girl back, someone who depends on you and thinks you're fabulous," I say.

And then we have a big fight.

Kristen

Dear Kristen:

Of course you're not jealous. Or defensive. But why not go to a nice supportive shrink just the same?

In the meantime, do not let Karen come home. I have seen children of famous parents, and it's not a pretty sight. One kid's father pulled a few strings and got him a big TV job right out of Harvard, paid for his apartment and gave him an allowance for a decade or two, and now the kid is in a fancy loony bin.

Kids with famous parents have varying degrees of delusions of grandeur. They've grown up around fabulous people, places and things, and assume this is normal. If you don't nip these kids in the bud, they become lost little snots who refuse to think they are fit for anything except a high-profile show-biz career.

But even if you weren't well known, even if you were well-off orthodontists, it doesn't pay to cushion a kid from actual life. A cushioned kid is a complacent kid. A complacent kid has no fear. Without fear you're nothing.

Problem Lady

Dear Problem Lady:

How come I never see a man drinking diet soda or using Equal? Do they think it's too girly or what? Some of them could sure use it.

Just Wondering

Dear Just:

Of course they think it's too girly! Worrying about your weight? About how you *look?* This would not be manly.

Conversely, how many women do we see drinking undiet soda or throwing sugar into their iced tea? Few, possibly none.

There are two reasons—

1. Peer pressure. A guy orders a Diet Sprite, say, and his friends will take that as an invitation to pee on his shoes. Drinking diet means you're not happy with your appearance, which anyone who aspires to being an alpha male may never admit. Even if he weighs three hundred pounds.

   Whereas your average woman, in order to keep peer approval, may never strut her stuff. She must always, even if she is a living strand, pretend she thinks she's fat and therefore *not a threat.* And if she *is* fat, well, that doesn't mean she's stupid. She knows what everyone will say the minute she goes to the ladies' room.

2. Men actually care much less about their appearance than women. So much so that they will not knowingly drink toxic chemicals.

Problem Lady

V

FALLING DOWN

20

LEAVING HOME

IT IS JULY 1997. JUST PAST MY FIRST WEDDING anniversary.

I have run away from home. I threw clothes into a suitcase, grabbed the dogs, got in my truck, drove to San Francisco. At first, I was really frightened. Whenever I went outside I kept falling, bumping my head on trees and poles, going blank. I couldn't decide what to do about my wedding ring. Put it on, take it off, repeat for an hour. It's *such* a beautiful ring, from Tiffany, too expensive, elegant.

Let me tell you about my marriage again. It had seemed so perfect. My husband and I became friends on the phone first. He

Originally appeared in *Playboy* magazine.

led me to believe he was a fat ugly soft pasty computer geek, so I thought, "Okay then, friends." When I saw him in the parking lot in front of the bookstore where we were to meet, I thought, "Damn, what a gorgeous brawny construction worker, if only *he* had brains."

Three weeks after we met he was picking me up at the airport. I got off the plane from New York and saw him standing with a huge bouquet of red roses and a tiny blue box. I got dizzy. He led me over to a chair in the waiting room, got down on his knees and proposed marriage.

"Yes," I said, yes, oh, absolutely yes I want to be married to you my wonderful dream man, no more confusing connections, no more rampant horniness, no more rejection agony, no more nauseous stomach of doomed expectations. You are smart, you are totally hilarious, you are beautiful. Absolutely. No doubt about it. Yes.

On my birthday my friend Bev got a party together fast. I wore my wedding ring. All these lovely San Francisco friends saying, "Happy Birthday! Where's that darling husband of yours?" I made up bright chirping lies. I put on a paper tiara.

I didn't marry him for money, or for fear of becoming a lonely old maid. I can't wait until the day that I am an old maid type, trolling through the Oxfordshire countryside with a pack of dogs and a wicked tongue. I fell in love with this man all the way to my reptilian brain.

We laughed and laughed. We squabbled over shelf space and forced one another to read favorite books. In the supermarket he liked to grab me and start fox-trotting. We each thought the other was madly sexy, even as I was putting on weight, then more weight. And got headaches. My cholesterol count rocketed out of control. And we laughed and laughed.

When I left him I went to a hotel in a tiny town at the edge of California. A hotel was the marriage counselor's idea. "When it gets like that, pick up your purse, go to a hotel," she said. The driving for seven hours was my own twist.

How do marriage counselors sleep at night, knowing all they know about marriage and not screaming it to the world? They should stand on their rooftops in their pajamas with a megaphone shouting, "Citizens! Never marry! Marriage is bad! Marriage is a bloodbath!"

But no, everyone keeps mum. No one tells about the sniping in the kitchen, the words like grenades flung across the bed, the radioactive silences in the rose garden. It's a big state secret that the merest ghost of a grimace of disapproval can cause cold blood rage.

My husband and I looked right into each other's souls and wanted to kill each other. I don't know why. I don't know how I ended up locking myself in the bathroom and puking into the toilet for the sake of love.

When I see into a beloved friend's soul I am full of affection, forgiveness, acceptance. But a beloved friend doesn't shriek with abandonment fear when you walk out the door. A beloved friend watches calmly as you go away for days, months. A beloved friend has no interest in scrutinizing your every action for a clue to secret betrayal.

It's the sex, of course. Primordial-ooze sex, the people's choice. The conspiracies of the selfish gene make the machinations of the military-industrial complex look like tic-tac-toe.

My cholesterol shot up so high my doctor was scared and sent me to a specialist. And so it was that I decided while I was in the cardiologist's office, while the technician was pasting electrodes all over my body, that perhaps this marriage wasn't working for me. My reptilian brain had a sudden new agenda: Get the fuck out, NOW.

I've rented myself a little cabin with actual thirty-year-old vinyl records. Right now I'm listening to The Band sing "The Shape I'm In." I feel okay. Well, awash with grief, but no longer insane and a danger to myself and others. I have walked on empty beaches staring at the shark-riddled ocean. I have discussed my life with ospreys and night herons, who are good listeners.

Women have of course taken over. They're feeding me, massaging me, giving me acupuncture and Chinese herbs, finding me places to stay and telling me to start crying already for God's sake or I'll never feel better.

The men have stayed politely in the background, the pharmacist solicitously filling my prescriptions, the mechanic silently changing a flat tire with a "She could blow at any time" demeanor.

It's been two weeks. Already, my jeans are looser. I am healing nicely. As soon as I'm better I am going to drive back into the city and get myself a honking huge tattoo of a snarling canine alpha bitch.

21

THE SEVENTIES

SUBURBIA 1971

I don't remember the first time I heard about that newfangled "Women's Liberation." I do remember a cover of *Life* magazine, something I think about Miss America and bras.

I didn't understand any of it. To me, the idea of women's equality had an unpleasantly shrewish ring to it. "Who needs *this?* This is too weird, buncha nuts, what's the matter with them?" were my thoughts.

I was busy playing housewife. Playing in earnest. I really believed I had settled into my life, with the baby carriages and the apartment in suburbia one thin mile away from my mother.

I knew of no alternatives. Hell, I didn't even know that you could be a mother and still have cool outfits! Or, for that matter, an actual life.

Was I depressed? You betcha. Did I even know it? No fucking way. I just thought life was lying in bed thinking dark thoughts and eating Oreo cookies day after day after day. I knew that as a housewife and a mother I was supposed to keep a spotless house and have other mothers over for coffee. But I couldn't seem to keep my house clean. I was constantly finding half-eaten sandwiches pushed under the bed and leaving them there.

None of my sketchy friendships with other mothers, formed mainly while taking my baby for a stroll around the apartment complex, seemed to go anywhere. The other mothers were probably just as depressed as I was. The biggest excitement I had was once my friend Jean and I, both nursing mothers, traded babies for a suckle. Woo-hoo, hold us back!

Can you even believe I was like this? I can't! You'd think that the very second I'd heard about it, I would have embraced feminism with open arms and stuck my tongue down its throat.

But, no, I was like a slave who had been emancipated but didn't want to leave the plantation.

It was safe and dull. We were so used to being marginalized, the humans who took care of the children and kept quiet during serious political discussions at cocktail parties, that anything else felt threatening.

So many women even expressed actual vitriolic hostility toward the radical feministas! Especially older women who had already dedicated a large portion of their lives to supporting and serving their men, women who felt that they had a lot to lose, women who had devoted their actual lives to a sweepingly false paradigm.

And you can't blame them. How would you feel if you had a horrible suspicion that your existence has perhaps all been pointless? The fear of annihilation would be so strong that you would go into deep denial and get pissed off at those who sought to set you free. You'd stick at home like a junkyard dog.

And then there's that pesky fear of being alone.

When feminism first started, men were not all *mea culpa.* They were furious. They felt betrayed. It got very nasty. They'd been working their butts off to support everybody, and this was how they were repaid? With anger and hatred?

Plus, it was kind of nice being treated as superior, nice having most of the power. Men didn't want to give that up, they didn't even understand the idea of giving it up, not at first. It took a while to sink in, just as it did with women. Men were not exactly cheerleading. In the beginning, feminists and men were sworn enemies. Obviously, many women were afraid that men would abandon them for feminist thinking.

Add to that the fear of not being able to take care of yourself in a world where people regard you as an incompetent ninny and you understand why feminism came first to college campuses, where students were free to express themselves while being supported by Mom and Dad.

But meanwhile, back in suburbia, I was getting bored to death. I had nowhere to wear my Betsey Johnson blue dress covered with the giant red cherries. I had nothing to look forward to except baby's first step and more Oreos.

I wasn't very far down that slippery scary road of making your man your everything. Although I had got to the hilarious our money/my money phase.

Steve, in 1970, made two hundred dollars a week as a radio announcer. This, to us, was big bucks, and this was *our* money. I had as much right to it as he did. Before I had a baby, I worked for a little hippie newspaper, where I made way less money, but that was *my* money. Maybe I would use it to buy us an air conditioner, or maybe I would take a solo trip to England, it was entirely up to me.

That was so not fair. Steve had virtually sole responsibility for both of us. No matter that he could command way more cash than I could, it still sucked. And I felt marginalized and discretionary like my income. We never actually talked about any of this. It's the way our parents did it, and their parents did it, it's just how it *was.*

Does it surprise you at all that we started talking to each other almost entirely in baby talk? We were strongly bonded yet completely unconscious while living a life that had nothing to do with us. We became infantile cookie-eaters.

But then, after three years of talking exactly like the little mice in Disney's *Cinderella,* Steve got a big job offer in Texas. We decided we would go. But first, I wanted to go to England. I'd read my Margaret Drabble, my Dickens, my Arthur Conan Doyle. I wanted to see 221B Baker Street. We decided Steve would go first, find us a place to live, I would join him in a month after my big European jaunt.

Our leave-taking was poignant. We spoke babee and we cried and hugged and cried again. Finally, he left. I heard the door slam. I was lying in bed as usual. But then the strangest thing happened.

I came to.

I remembered who I was. It all came back in a huge flood of feeling:

The miserable kid in suburbia who ran away to the big city, stifled by her life with her parents, trying to be goofy and weird and arty. How had this happened? What did I think I was doing, living back here a mile away from my mother?

I lay there until it became dark. Then I got up and put on my Betsey Johnson cherry outfit and brushed my hair. I spent the evening in the living room—out of bed, for once—dancing with my baby to Rod Stewart's "Maggie May." And thinking about women's lib.

LONDON 1972

Six months later I was sitting in a consciousness-raising group in a slum in South London, talking about masturbation.

I was now a legal squatter in a derelict house in South London. There were nine of us, four architectural students fixing up the house, two "unsupported mothers," and three very tiny children. Sometimes we would overhear the children discussing "Happily Ever After," and we would yell at them to cut it out. It was heavenly, even if I did see my breath every morning in the winter and even if I did have to put pennies in the gas meter. I had a lover named George. Hi George!

Steve was beginning to believe I was not coming back. What I did to him was awful. I got to England, realized this was the world for me, felt wide awake, and just couldn't see going back.

I worked as a community organizer for a South London community center and became a big activist. I'd read all possible Saul Alinsky books, *Rules for Radicals* was my favorite. I was against social workers for trying to make people fit the system and for changing society to fit people instead. I was all vehement.

I read Simone de Beauvoir's *The Second Sex* and it scared me to death. I read a feminist magazine called *Spare Rib.* And I read Germaine Greer's *The Female Eunuch.*

This consciousness-raising group really did consciousness-raise. We could talk about anything.

"How do you do it?" I asked. "This masturbation stuff."

"Cynthia, you're kidding," Gillian said. Then she looked at me, realized I wasn't.

"Well, you know what you do with your fingers," said Jenny.

"I do," I said. "But nothing happens."

"You've got to think of things," said Sue. "Like doing it with someone you really fancy."

"Like in a forbidden place," said Gillian.

"Make up a whole story in your head," said Ann.

I couldn't wait to get home and try, but we still had other things to talk about. Like how we had collapsed into giggles trying to look at our cervixes with cosmetics mirrors the week before. Like how all the men got the good jobs, like why the married men hit on us all the time. Like being called dear, and girlie, and honey.

"We're just as good as the men, really, aren't we?" asked Gillian.

"We're better," said Jenny.

"I wouldn't go that far," I said, secretly thrilled.

"I would," said Jenny. "They're a bunch of conceited bastards with no empathy and no clue how to go about living in the world without women looking after them."

This kind of talk excited us madly. It seemed so . . . so *illicit!*

We each came to the meeting alone, but by the end of the evening we were a group with gestalt. We were bigger, and more relieved, and happier, than the sum of our parts.

It was the sisterhood. Sisterhood really *was* powerful. It took us out of ourselves and put us into something big and shining and free. It made us laugh and open our hearts.

Because we sisters only had each other. We worked as a group against herculean resistance. Not only did men not like us and women feel deeply suspicious, but there were no society sanctions. The media made fun of us. No governments had jumped on the bandwagon. Corporations wanted us dead. Women's liberation was still an underground movement.

So we changed it all, one mind at a time.

It all seems so different now. Sisterhood is no longer quite so necessary, and can even be a trap. Women have come so far that they now are just as likely to be big assholes as any man. There are few secret smoldering looks of solidarity and understanding between women anymore, not like during the sisterhood heyday.

I kind of miss it.

NEW YORK 1975

Ms. Germaine Greer was coming to the Population Institute! As the secretary in the entrance foyer, I would be the first to meet and greet her!

I felt that I almost couldn't breathe I was so overexcited! She would notice me, we could talk of this and that, I could tell her how she changed my life, we could trade stories of sexism thwarted and have a good old feminist laugh!

Finally she wafted in, all tall, willowy and beautiful. He eyes swept over me as if I weren't there. I said hello and I saw her register it but she didn't answer me, she just swept toward the male directors with outstretched hands.

Well.

Thanks for writing *The Female Eunuch,* Germaine Greer, but here's a poke in the eye for making me feel like shit.

A couple of weeks later, the crotchety old director wanted me to write an important letter.

"You're the creative type," he said. "Write a creative business letter."

My head spun around like Linda Blair's, an unholy noise came from my throat, and I was out of there.

I had nothing to do but start writing.

VI

A NEW LEASH

22

LIFE: A THEME PARK

AT ABOUT 3:30 A.M. HELICOPTERS STARTED CIRCLING the house and tore me out of my soggy, jet-lagged sleep. Searchlights were blazing, radios blared. Drooling and stupid, it never occurred to me to grab a baseball bat or an Uzi in case some hardened criminal smashed the window. No, I thought I was on TV. Some cop show, maybe.

I guess I could blame my idiocy on Oxfordshire, where I had just spent over a month in the tiny village of Middle Twee.

Ah, Middle Twee! So luscious and green and cute and thatched! So idyllic and peaceful and cricket-playing! Cows mooing in meadows! Baby lambs frolicking! Pigs and dogs snuffling! No helicopters whatsoever!

When I first arrived in this jewel of a village, I thought, "Well here I am in *Howards End.*" I put on a long skirt like Vanessa Redgrave and strode along, trailing my fingers through tendrils of leaves, sniffing the air, making sure my hair cascaded. I took to the tiny lanes and lost myself in reveries and stumbled right smack into an elderly couple in bright pink sweatsuits.

"Isn't this just so *sweet,* so *pretty*!" said the wife. "We think it's like *Howards End,* don't we dear?"

"I'll never understand those damned f-stops," said the husband, wielding his camera at some particularly browbeaten thatch and letting forth a fusillade of shots.

Back at the village green I saw that the place was swarming with dozens of identical sweatsuited couples, recently emerged from a gleaming silver tour bus. I was livid. It was all spoiled. I was in a tourist trap. I retreated into my borrowed cottage, only emerging to drive five miles to the nearest fish-and-chip shop or to try and make friends with a big black dog who ambled around with such a tone that I was convinced he was the mayor.

That was week one. By week two I became adept at parading around in my underwear, which scared off most of the elderly couples who were peering, cameras at the ready, through my window. The rest I managed to peel off my gate by singing Sex Pistols tunes.

After all, I knew how to live in a theme park. I lived in Greenwich Village for fifteen years. Greenwich Village, Bohemian paradise in the twenties, thirties, forties, fifties. Somewhere around 1968 it became the theme park version of itself, teeming with suburban tourists of all ages intent on rubbing elbows with artists and hippies and drinking that weird espresso coffee. By

1992 it had descended into a theme park for drunks and drug addicts, and like the rest of the residents I knew better than to ever expect to see a parking space or to leave my house at all on weekends, and I was enormously skilled at sidestepping teeming pools of fresh vomit and eluding the octopus grasps of delirious crackheads. That's when I finally left.

So Middle Twee was a piece of cake. But I was getting lonely. There were people who, by their absence of sweatsuits and cameras, I figured actually lived in the village, but they barely nodded to me. The black dog ignored me in a regal manner. So I tramped around for hours, getting giddy from smelling cow parsley and weeds, feeling too peaceful, fixed in time and space.

At the beginning of week three I marched up to the woman who worked in the only shop. "Is that your black dog?" I asked.

"Yes," she said, "come have a cup of tea." And that was that. I was plucked from the glossy surface into the village underground! I was suddenly spending all my indoor time in kitchens in the backs of houses or behind Ye Olde Creame Tea Shoppes, behind doors and curtains where the villagers hid from the sweatsuited throngs. The dog, Worcestershire, let me pat his head. I caught the thread of all the gossip and hung on for dear life.

Have you noticed movies lately? Bad, of course, but always finding new ways to be bad. Movies ineptly try to provide whatever is missing for the human psyche. Thus the many *caring, loving* movies. Thus the movies where the hero actually gets to blow the bad guy's brains out. And lately we've got movies full of *land.* Awe-inspiring scenery that leaves us breathless and yearning for we know not what.

We've lost touch with the earth, the earth we crave with our DNA. We lose ourselves at the movies or descend upon unsuspecting villages with Leicas.

By week four, Worcestershire the dog had moved in with me. I was immersed in all the gossip about the vicar's housekeeper. Only trouble was, most of the people who actually lived there were in imminent danger of losing their farms and houses to Londoners looking for a quaint weekend getaway. It had gotten so bad there was a suicide hotline for farmers. But never mind, it's pretty. It's *Howards End.*

By week five I was back, under the helicopters, missing the sweet countryside like mad. Goddammit, I'm in the wrong movie.

23

MY ANGEL HOMER

LET ME START OUT WITH AN OPEN LETTER TO THE MAN who dumped a medium-sized beagle-ish red elderly dog out of his car at a strip mall in Moorpark, California, in the spring of 1992.

Dear Disgusting Lump of Putrid Slime:

You are going to rot forever in hell. As fire ants slowly eat your eyeballs, vipers will crawl down your throat and devour your entrails. Satan himself will spit on you in disgust.

And the dogs will laugh.

My dog Homer was stubborn and loyal. When he got dumped in front of that strip mall, he held his post for over a week, keeping out of human reach, refusing even tender pig ears from his would-be rescuers in order to continue his vigil. He was that sure someone would be back for him.

But finally he got too hungry and let himself be caught. He was eleven years old. He spent six months in an excellent no-kill animal shelter where he sat listlessly and hopelessly. Then I came and got him and brought him home and put him on the couch and fed him cheese and it was good.

Dogs are all about love. But they are not about human-style love, so you don't need to wear mascara or do the tango. The more unwashed we are, the more they dote on us.

Here's a very important fact if we want to get the most from our doggie relationships: Dogs are not "inferior." Dogs are not pets. Also, dogs are not human. If we regard our pups as this cute widdle wuzzums on whom to put darling tiny costumes, we'll never learn a thing of any use to anybody.

A dog has the complement of our senses. Dogs are all about body language and smell. And pure innocence.

Homer was a plain ole dog, no frills, no pedigree at all, just essence of K-9, which, if you ask me, is at least next to godliness. Look into a dog's eyes, especially your own dog's eyes, and you will see infinite trust, crazy trust. It took Homer about three minutes to actually trust me after he was discarded like a used Kleenex. I looked into his eyes and saw my own version of religion.

Plus he had that pungent doggie smelliness. I sniffed at his feet and swooned with happiness.

I bought him a $180 collar from Harrods in London. I fed him the human grade–ingredient dog food and he had the best supplements and bottled water. He had a hand-knit wool coat for chilly days. I watched as his coat turned from broken and dull to glossy and thick, as he lost his extra weight and began running at the park. I loved to watch my Homer run. He would smile every second, he never wanted to stop. His fave game was to make me run after him until I shrieked with frustration.

He was scared of thunder and hid in the closet. Even lavish hugs, even treats, couldn't console him. Otherwise he spent his days angling for cookies. He loved when I gave parties. I would watch him casually amble up to guests and then *snatch* the food off their plates faster than the eye could see.

Once he greeted me at the door with a potato chip bag over his entire head. Inside the bag he was still inhaling crumbs.

I asked the fabric of God and the forces of the universe to let me have a year with him. He was so smiley, so *dogged.*

After two years his arthritis was starting to bother him. Once or twice he screamed when he tried to stand up. It was horrid hearing Homer cry. I gave him Rimadyl, an anti-inflammatory drug for dogs, and a glucosamine/chondroitin cocktail, and took him for acupuncture. And he got better and life again was jolly.

After a particularly rainy winter, my back gate became so swollen that I just jammed it closed. What I didn't know is that wood shrinks again in the sun, and gates swing open. One morning a neighbor came to my back door and told me my brown dog was out, running around the neighborhood.

"I don't have a brown dog, I have a *red* dog," I said.

"Whatever," he said.

I ran outside in my nightgown and an entire battalion of neighbors, some who lived as far as three streets away, were chasing Homer, who was wearing his poncy Harrods collar and a brown cableknit sweater and trotting hither and thither, eating random morsels of cat shit. I ran to him and shouted and he threw himself into my arms, thrilled to death with his excellent adventure. The neighbors applauded as if it were a movie.

After four years Homer went semideaf. He wasn't scared of thunder or fireworks anymore, he couldn't hear them. He started watching me, following me around the house, needing security. I installed a sofa in each room, he loved a nice sofa. If he couldn't make the jump himself I hoisted him and he would snarfle the way dogs do when they're pleased. Smiley-dog!

I've said it before but it bears repeating: Old dogs are the best! So civilized, over that pesky chewing period, too dignified to hump legs. Adopting an old dog is not only a mitzvah, it's a downright pleasure.

We lived through earthquakes, floods, sickness and health and the day-to-day tedium that dogs love. This past year Homer was looking frail, his coat was white, he couldn't jump into the car, he couldn't even jump on his beloved sofas. The acupuncture and daily massages helped a lot. He never cried anymore, but watching him lower himself from a standing position to lie down hurt my heart.

But he smiled, and trotted around a little more slowly, still stole food whenever possible. I bought a little tent at a pet store for my smaller dogs. Homer loved that tent, kept trying to wedge himself in it, kept getting stuck. So I got him a child-sized tent at IKEA. He was so pleased. He would herd me into the office so he could lie in his tent, bolstered by many cushions, king of all he surveyed.

My last picture of him shows him looking out from his blue tent, smiling big time.

One Sunday he couldn't get up. His gums were white. He panted. My son and I fashioned a stretcher from towels and a sheet and carried him with us everywhere. We got chicken from Homer's favorite, El Pollo Loco, and even in his weakened state he gobbled it up. I held him and crooned to him for twenty-four hours and then we took him to the car. I fed him chicken skin while we drove to the vet. The vet came to the car and while I kissed Homer and sang in the high-pitched voice he could still hear and gave him more chicken the vet injected him with barbiturates and Homer died.

The scum-sucking pig who dumped my Homer by the side of the road inadvertently gave Homer and me the great gift of finding each other. The lovely smell of him will stay with me forever. He was my happiness, my angel boy.

24

DOG IS MY COPILOT

I HAD TO GO TO A WEDDING IN NEW YORK, BUT I CAME a week early so I could see the Border collies.

My old neighborhood has become a mall: Hold Everything, Pottery Barn, Barnes and Noble, Bed, Bath and Blow Me.

After walking down Seventh and watching Duracell people powered up and gleaming mad, I felt the Dog Need. In the past few years my DNA has altered. All cells reach toward dogitude. I need dog breath, eyes, fur, smell. And dogs notice. Even on Seventh Avenue, dogs pulled at their leads to jump, wriggle, kiss, sniff, smile at me. Whereas the dogs' humans fretted. "He bites," they'd say as their Akitas rolled over for me to rub their stomachs. Okay I'm bragging but it just kills me.

I walked up to Madison Square Garden, passing dogs who twirled gleefully at my approach, prostrated themselves before me, constructed rawhide shrines in my wake. I very casually strolled past the block-long lines and oozed up to the ticket window, bought a ticket for the Westminster Kennel Club annual dogfest, the biggest and classiest dog show in America. Dog show to the stars. All champion dogs. Hot stuff. The American Kennel Club's finest hour.

"It's fixed, we know it's fixed, why do we bother entering?" asked the woman behind me.

I trotted up to ring eight, just in time to see the papillons competing. They marched in circles and submitted to the judge's inquiring hand on their balls. I thought about my two rescued papillons. One, half an inch too big to be a show dog, sat alone in a cage for his first seven months. He's the one who tries to lick nostrils. The other was used as a canine football and still snaps and trembles.

I went looking for the Border collies but couldn't locate them because I couldn't move. People were crammed together, snapping, grabbing free samples of food, shopping for dog watches, earrings. The dogs themselves were nearly invisible. The Westminster show is a benched show, meaning the dogs can't leave. They mainly stay in their little cubicles in crates, are taken to a square of sawdust to eliminate.

As I got pushed along I studied the dogs. A Pekingese in a tiny box was whining pitifully. A basset tried to stick her nose through the grate in her crate. These were the dogs in good shape. The rest of them were catatonic. So stressed, they were in shock. I passed frozen greyhounds, rigid poodles, Bernese mountain dogs in crates too small to stand or turn around. They looked half dead. Some had to be rushed out to the arena before they collapsed from the heat.

And this, this is the American Kennel Club's finest hour. The AKC, an alleged snakepit of politics and petty rivalries. The AKC, which could stop the atrocity of puppy mills but does fuck-all because it's so fond of registration fees.

I passed a Chow Chow waiting to go into the ring. "Your scarf is touching his coat!" his handler shrieked.

I had a cigarette with a Bernese breeder. "Of course it's fixed," she said. "The judges have their favorites. I mean, everyone knows the Clumber's going to win. How do they all know if it isn't fixed?"

I watched the papillon win the toy group. His owners and handler were thrilled to bits. They shoved the dog in a tiny crate and went to have a drink. I crouched down to say hello to the gorgeous little dog. He was quaking.

I heard many more people complaining that the show was fixed. What I think they meant was that it's all about who you know, who handles your dog and how much money you've spent campaigning for your darling creature.

Finally I saw the Border collies. This incredible breed is the genius of the canine species, a dog who should never be a pet because if she isn't working and running all day she'll eat your entire front door. Border collies hypnotize sheep with their "eye," a stare so intense and dominating a cougar would be cowed into submission. Border collie lovers tried to stop the

AKC from recognizing the breed, they didn't want the dogs ruined by sacrificing temperament and health to the AKC's rigid "standards."

The three Border collies, confined for hours in their small crates, were listless. Their famous eyes were dull, dead, glazed with depression. It was a brutal, nauseating sight. I went home and entertained fantasies of the Border collies gathering all their brethren and staging a siege, herding all the humans into tiny cages and making them pee on sawdust and parade in circles while having their genitals examined.

I had bad dreams and decided not to go back for the second day of doggie torture.

But I did go back. The Clumber won Best in Show. Go figure.

25

TAKE MY COLLECTIBLES, PLEASE

COME INTO MY LOVELY HOME. THAT'S OKAY, JUST KICK those boxes aside. They arrive every day, deliveries from my ebay raids. Careful of the box marked "fragile," it's probably the rare McCoy gun dog bookend that I bid an insane amount of money on. I bet I don't even like it. Nevertheless, I must own every McCoy pottery dog item that exists.

No, silly, I don't need every *living* dog. It just seems like a lot when you first open the door, but there are only six. Look how they like you! Oh sorry about that, I *must* remember to trim their nails. Are you sure you're all right?

Why yes, I *do* have a lot of pottery. See that big yellow bowl with the flower border? That's Rookwood. I got it at auction for only $60. I'm sick to death of it. I'd like to smash it on the floor and jump on the pieces. I know it's a lovely bowl, but the pottery has taken over my house. Someday I'll come home and the pottery will be watching TV and smoking cigarettes. Plus pottery is so needy! It wants dusting, it wants arranging, it wants little butterfly kisses.

I remember how it all started. Somebody had brought me roses. I had no vase. I went to Pier One and the vases were all over thirty dollars and rather horrid. I thought I'd buy an antique vase instead.

Do you enjoy the feeling of luxurious anticipation that wafts over you when you convince yourself you *must* buy a decorative item? I turned it into a major project. I went to dozens of yard sales and antique malls over the next couple of weeks. Soon I had three McCoy vases: A matte green vase (*McCoy Pottery: Collector's Reference and Value Guide,* page 136, right). A hyacinth form (page 167). A rustic jardiniere (page 217).

I was in love. McCoy pottery, I felt, was the bee's knees. I would see a nice early Nelson McCoy butterfly vase and go all weak and blush. It was hard to parse the feeling, but I think it was an amalgam of place and time nostalgia.

Here I was in beastly Los Angeles, but I am a Pennsylvania girl born and bred. I miss the hills. I miss the colors. I *really* miss the shapes of the foliage. McCoy pottery was made in Zanesville, Ohio, from 1848 to 1990. It looks like Pennsylvania. I look at a McCoy pot and I think of early spring when I was a child visiting the great-aunts. It's a musty, fusty, gorgeous feeling. I made a pilgrimage to Zanesville once and stared hungrily at the trees.

One day it all stopped. McCoy left me unfulfilled. Even the mustiest, fustiest of all, the dark brown and floral Loy-Nel-Art, paled. I have to say I felt a little bereft.

But never mind, like a spider plant, my collecting obsession had little, perfectly formed babies and I started collecting bark cloth, seventies clothing by Willi Smith, Perry Ellis, Stephen Burrows and Patrick Kelly. And handbags of any sort as long as insane.

Here, let me take you to the guest room, where the clothes and handbags reside. See this Patrick Kelly white piqué jacket with the giant musical notes? Three dollars, Goodwill! See these purses that are also telephones? On the cover of Sotheby's *Nothing to Wear* catalog! See these Norma Kamali seventies-era sweats? Are they a collection, or just old clothes?

I don't wanna talk about the dogs.

Okay, I'll talk about the dogs.

I had a dinner party once and someone came up to me and said, "You have a *great* collection of dog art."

She could have been sincere, she could have been mocking, since I only had a few pictures and the odd Rookwood figurine. But I took these words as a challenge, the throwing down of the glove.

As I'm sure you can see from the incredibly disorganized tangle of Scottie bookends, fifties-era photos of fox terriers, Royal Doulton flag-draped bulldogs, the dog-festooned oil paintings, watercolors and pencil sketches, tea towels, dresser caddies, Syrocco tie racks, light switches, hand-painted neckties, planters, and, okay, the crocheted toilet paper cover shaped like a poodle. My favorites are, of course, the dog bark cloth and the McCoy dogs (cross-collecting!).

But, please believe me, I never did buy that dog-shaped teakettle, or the reproduction iron pointer-shaped nutcracker. And you will please make note that I do not, and never will, have the front of my house festooned with dog flags. I am nothing if not tasteful.

Here, sit down. Tuck this pug needlepoint cushion into the small of your back. I will make you Fortnum's tea in this stunning McCoy teapot. (Yes, my McCoy interest is piquing again, although it does feel a lot like a nostalgia for nostalgia, which is a little too postmodern to bear.)

Take it all. I'll give you a good price. Rock-bottom bargain-basement time. Sell it, break it, just get it out of my sight. I don't want to have to look at it anymore.

No, sorry, not the Wodehouse first editions. Not the Bob Dylan bootlegs or the obscure punk rock records. I'm sorry, no! These are things that take me into other worlds, they're still alive. Like the world of my living dogs, who teach me the heady pleasures of butt-sniffing and couch-wriggling.

This other stuff, this stuff you must buy from me before I go stark staring loony, is only alive when I'm prowling for it, when it's out of reach and tantalizing. The Weller planter that bobs and weaves from a high shelf in an antique shop? When I bring it home it flops, gasps, dies.

I think I'm the human version of the polar bear pacing back and forth back and forth at the zoo. I'm hunting and gathering, hunting and gathering, in this horrible city that casually suffocates.

I've gotta get out of here. I'm moving to the country, or at least Oakland. And I *don't* want to pack.

Of course I'll keep buying stuff on ebay, I don't think anyone in the world could kick *that* habit, but instead of keeping it, let me send it to you.

Please?

26

LITTLE ANNIE, HAPPY AT LAST

THE LATEST ADDITION TO OUR PACK IS A YOUNG DOG named Annie. She's only visiting, recuperating from abuse. You think you know all about abuse until you hear what happened to this Benji-cute, blue-eyed, schnauzer-colored bitch.

She was a stray, wandering hither and thither, when she shit on the wrong woman's lawn. This woman's son, visiting from Vegas and brimming with filial devotion, set his pit bull on Annie. But the pit bull simply didn't have the stomach for it, maybe he liked the blue eyes. So the son did the only logical thing. He put a bag over Annie's head, poured gasoline all over her body, and set her on fire.

Neighbor children screamed, police and animal control officers arrived. Annie was taken to a city shelter.

She was in a cage with third-degree burns and without medical attention for a week. If no one claims an animal after a week, she is euthanized (that's if the animal is a stray; if her "owner" turns her in, she is euthanized within hours). A worker at the shelter called the local bleeding heart, a woman named June, and asked if she wanted to adopt Annie before she was killed.

"She was so badly burned and in such pain she could only walk sideways like a crab, but even then she leaned against me and asked for a cuddle," said June. "My vet said there was no way she'd live. She said even a pit bull couldn't survive."

Hah. This chick, this thin little raggedy-assed bitch, is thriving. She's had six months of skin grafts and then developed what Lyssa, the dog trainer, calls "rescue dog monster syndrome." They're sick, they're sick, they're coddled and indulged, they get better, they get better still, and before their humans know it they think they rule the world.

Doc, the big Lab/shepherd who rules the pack with an iron paw, developed a grudging crush on Annie. He wanted to make sure she realized his magnificence. He caught his red squeaky ball with splendid grace when she was around.

"If you're such a big deal," she must have said in dog lingo as she chewed on a pen, a twenty-dollar bill, and the TV remote all at once, "open the goddamned refrigerator door. Come on. There's an entire chicken in there!"

"Piece o' cake," Doc must've said back. He set his mind to it, he did it. The humans got home to find no chicken, no cheese, empty yogurt containers, grapes strewn around in frustration for being only grapes.

The humans went insane and put all kinds of child locks and Velcro on the fridge door. This worked fine until Annie went into heat. (No one knew! Not even the Ur-vet could tell if she were spayed! And it's dangerous to spay them until the heat is over!)

All bets were off. The dogs went mental. A female in heat! We must all forget we are housebroken! We must whine and hide under beds and bark at nothing! We must regress and eat shoes!

Doc suddenly figured out how to open the child locks, rip off the Velcro and duct tape, move chairs. He didn't even mind the "Snappy-trainers," which resemble mousetraps and snap loudly when touched. The humans were beside themselves. The dogs didn't care.

Then Annie tried to get Doc to have sex with her. So what that he was neutered! She wanted it, she wanted it now!

She paraded her butt before him, the tail curled to the side enticingly. When he didn't respond, she jumped on his head and barked. Then he'd lie down. Then she'd lie down on top of him. He'd walk away. She'd mount him. Paw at his face.

And so he had sex with her. Neutered dogs have sex all the time.

Well, not all the time. Doc was embarrassed. His precious dignity had come undone. He tried to ignore Annie after a couple of couplings. But she kept at him. Meanwhile, the show dog schnauzer next door, inflamed and intact, kept escaping and knocking on our door. The dachshund bitch who lives with the schnauzer wanted Annie dead.

She finished her heat cycle. Doc was so relieved. The schnauzer couldn't believe it. He kept at her, trying and trying to hump her, and each time she showed him her teeth and threatened to beat the shit out of him. She is my hero.

She is spayed now, of course, and she lives in Berkeley. She has her own house, her own yard, her own pet dog, and even her own human, Ernie, to watch over her. It was discovered that she is very likely a Berger des Pyrénées, a fancy French breed. She has the longest, silkiest silver hair and everyone stops to pay court to her.

Just like they should to every dog.

27

POLITICAL CORRECTION

I THOUGHT THE GUY WAS GONNA HAVE A STROKE. WHEN I got out of my car I saw him standing on his front lawn brushing his teeth, and clocked him as Bay Area kooky. "Lemme show you something," he said and walked toward my front porch. He pointed under a bush at a small cardboard box containing one balled-up newspaper, two beer bottles, and a Diet Coke can.

"That's been there since the day you moved in," he said. "Do you want me to call the Department of Health? Oh, and also, that vehicle that you drive? Do you know what it does to the air? Have you thought about the height of the bumper? Do you know what you can do to a neighbor's car? And don't put trash on the corner. Don't tell *me* that's not yours! Of course it's yours! Do you want me to throw it over your fence?"

Well.

Pretty soon there was yelling and I said lots of words like "Go fuck yourself" before I stomped into my house and waited half an hour for my heart to leave my throat.

So I just want to say I'm sorry! I have an SUV! I didn't know they were wrong! I'm sorry for everything, in fact! Please, everybody in San Francisco, stop being angry with me about everything!

Everybody told me that the Bay Area is all madly mellow. Buncha hippies and all that. NO! Everywhere I go, there is anger. There are people demanding their rights! A citizens' group in Berkeley is furious because a synagogue might be built on *too small a parcel of land!* I find this almost insane. At the Richard Thompson show at the Fillmore the other night, a clump of revelers became irate that the pictures on the wall were not "multicultural" enough, and I'm not at all sure they were kidding. A massive feeling of entitlement courses through the citizenry's blood. Probably because it costs so much to live here. You pay through the nose, you want it perfect, goddammit!

I've just moved from LA. I'm still getting used to things. In LA no one is mad at anyone. Everyone is constantly sunny and friendly as they cut your heart right out of your chest. Plus, in LA I had a Saab! Really! I was very correct, but then, with six dogs, I got a Land Rover. I didn't know it was wrong and evil. I thought it was cool and British. In LA you practically must have a Jeep Grand Cherokee, so I was a rebel.

Before that, in Manhattan, we didn't know from cars. Or, for that matter, porches or lawns or neighbors. In Manhattan we knew to put our trash out once a week and to avoid urine puddles on the subway, period.

I've been in Oakland for three months. It is wonderful. There are plenty of people with no face-lifts whatsoever and I actually heard people in a restaurant talking about a Nancy Mitford book. Many people look and act like me to the point where I have discovered that I am a type. I found a great (Harvard graduate!!) garden designer, who, after I explained for a good twenty minutes about the kind of garden I wanted, stopped me and said, "Oh, I get it. You want a hipster garden." I am a hipster. I'm so proud.

However I do note that people here—like my toothbrushing neighbor—are just a teensy bit tense. And I wonder, is driving like a maniac the best way to assuage this? I totally understand being annoyed on the freeways at the constantly disappearing right lane and what the *hell* is that about? The incessant merging left is really fraught with irritation, yes, but, jeez, why take it out on me?

What, exactly, is *wrong* with San Franciscans using blinkers to change lanes? Is it considered de trop? Personally, I hate it when I'm driving along and suddenly a blue Mazda is up my nose. And why, when some poor dork from out of town *does* use her blinker, is it interpreted as a signal for every car in her desired lane to *speed up*? And why, when this poor driver tries to give you the hairy eyeball, does everyone *refuse to make eye contact*? Are they chicken? Face up to the hairy eyeballs, dammit!

Maybe they would drive like this in Los Angeles if they could get away with it, but with traffic congealing for hours because of one false swerve, with road disputes settled with firearms, LA drivers are polite and efficient, or dead.

LA drivers know nothing of crosswalks, though; pedestrians run like startled rabbits in even the most sedate of neighborhoods. Here people vehemently know their rights, especially on Piedmont Avenue in Oakland, where I am a constant nervous wreck. It seems that the entire length of Piedmont is a pedestrian crossing. People dart out from behind parked cars and glare haughtily! People step off the curb without looking at all! I have heard a whole lot of screaming by pedestrians, one woman gave me the finger when she crossed against a red light, one man started beating fiercely on a Chevy Caprice that was traveling through a crosswalk at inches per minute.

Let me again reiterate that I love it here, okay? Because I've noticed that what makes the Bay Area most irate is daring to say that New York may be more interesting, or prettier, or, God forbid, more relevant. I didn't know until I got here that we are indeed at the center of the universe. I thank my lucky stars that you let me in! Love it here, I do!

I adore the treatment of talkers during movies. In New York if you even give a half turn and an eye roll, you're going to get, "What the fuck are *you* looking at?" In LA you get the morons clapping at the names in the credits so people think they know somebody. Here, silence is enforced with surly fury by the majority and there is much submissive slinking.

I'm nuts about the jolly chattiness in supermarket lines, where people will give you recipes and life histories.

And the best thing in all the Bay Area is the dog park at Point Isabel. It is sheer heaven, it fills my soul with quiet joy. My beautiful Lab/shepherd, Doc, has memorized every rock and path and frolics unreservedly even though he is as blind as any bat. And hardly anyone gets annoyed at my Lab/Dobie Prunella, who must wear a muzzle due to her profound dislike of all white and fluffy dogs. Prunella likes to go swimming and rub madly against every human crotch she can find, her way of pleading for someone/anyone to remove her muzzle. Everybody just laughs hahaha!

But even here, in Mecca, there is anger. "You're a breedist!" a woman said to my friend Ernie, who has Annie. Just because she might be a fancy breed.

And I must say I was shocked, *shocked,* at the woman in the Rabat shoe store on Fourth Street in Berkeley, which is the most excellent shoe shop maybe ever, who went into a hissy-fit because Mikey sniffed her ankle. Mikey is a little rescued papillon who wouldn't hurt a flea. The very well groomed woman accused him of *licking*! "Please be aware that not everyone enjoys a dog licking her! Can't you have better control over your animals?" she said as she stomped out on unpleasant shoes.

Another day I was with my dogs in what I thought was the leash-free dog park in the Berkeley Marina, only to be told by a foul-tempered man that I wasn't.

"The leash-free area is over that hill!" he yelled. I said okay. He wasn't happy.

"Hey, get your dogs on a leash, get them on a leash now, right now! You're breaking the rules! Why can't you follow the rules?" he screamed and screamed.

I'd had *enough.* I went over to him and stood with my face an inch from his. "I didn't know that I wasn't in the proper dog park," I hissed really low. "I would never knowingly break any of your rules."

I took a step toward him. He took a step back. I advanced. He retreated. I considered decking him. He considered me decking him.

"Get away from me, you . . . you . . . bitch!" he shouted and ran away.

I love it here, I really do. But I'm *so* glad I'm from New York.

28

A VERY MODERN WEDDING

YOU COULD ACTUALLY CALL THE WEDDING PARTY "LOVELY." The pretty bride and the handsome groom were dressed with casual elegance. They graciously welcomed their friends to their tasteful West Los Angeles house. Everything sparkled in the tea lights. Pot stickers and calamari sat on the gleaming dining table.

The tanned young guests in their best trendy clothes arrived in a bunch. They brought flowers and gifts, bottles of nice wine, champagne. They were friendly and jokey, heartfelt congratulations were expressed with big hugs and kisses. True, it wasn't a fancy party, there was no band or brouhaha, just soft music, warm conversation and, oh yeah, MTV blaring.

Because soon, in just a couple of minutes, the assembled guests were going to be crowding around the TV set, watching the lovely couple get married in their bathing suits on MTV's game show, *I Got Married During Spring Break.* Las Vegas's only ordained Elvis impersonator would be officiating.

Everybody blames the parents, but I swear I was against this. "Are you sure you want your wedding to be a sideshow?" I asked my son, Brodie, beforehand—not much beforehand, I'd only had three days' notice.

"That's fine with us," said Brodie. "Adriane and I love each other, who cares how we get married? Plus, if we actually do win, we get a free honeymoon in Cancún!"

Kids. What are you gonna do?

I mentioned to him the last couple to get married on TV, that horrid twisted millionaire couple. Didn't matter. I mentioned the less-than-romantic timbre the proceedings would take. No dice. I worried vociferously about MTV humiliating them—a game show in their bathing suits, forsooth!

"We know our boundaries," Brodie said. "They can't push us over them." Hahahahahahaha.

A thrill ran through the party. Brodie turned on the video camera so that he would have a tape of his friends watching his pretaped wedding. Everyone grabbed their drinks and gathered. The bride sat in the center of the sofa, flanked by her best girlfriends, staring at the TV screen. It was time.

No, wait! Suddenly we had to watch Jerry Springer cavorting on a beach while some guy wrote with lipstick on a young woman's naked butt. Then, it was really time.

There were four engaged couples. Brodie and Adriane were

the yellow couple, he in yellow swim shorts, she in a modest yellow bikini with a bit of yellow net hanging from her hair.

First the blindfolded groom had to recognize his bride's kiss as opposed to the kiss of one of the Barbie Twins. Everybody guessed right.

Then everybody had to root around in a pool filled with different-sized balloons to find the balloon that roughly corresponded to the prospective bride's cup size. Everybody got wet—woohoo! We saw Adriane holding up balloons and carefully studying her own breasts. "They made me do that!" she shouted above the hoots.

Couples were eliminated in random fashion.

For the *pièce de résistance,* one of each remaining couple had to be smeared with cake and frosting, which was then licked off by the other. You could say it looked obscene, and I do. Brodie was smeared, Adriane licked. The party-goers went mad. I looked at Adriane. She had disappeared. Oh there she was, slunk down into a puddle of humiliated, embarrassed girl on the sofa, hidden by her protective bridesmaids.

When they won, they were led, still covered with frosting, up to the Elvis impersonator. My son looked precisely like The Mummy. Adriane looked like Audrey Hepburn caught in the headlights. Getting married covered with cake is probably not as easy as it looks.

Would we call this wedding a travesty?

We could, but look at traditional wedding customs. "Giving the bride away" is still widely practiced. Carrying her over the threshold is a ritual directly descended from the rape of the Sabine women. The thousands of dollars spent by the bride's parents for the wedding reception is the modern version of bestowing a dowry. This is not sacrament, this is marketplace.

Modern sacrament and dignity, if found anywhere, would be at a pretension-free simple ceremony at City Hall. Especially since they never, ever lead in with Jerry Springer.

29

PROBLEM LADY

Dear Problem Lady:

My friend, or kind of a friend anyway, well, I guess she's my friend, anyway she's in the hospital. And I have her dog.

It's been three months now. Susie, who's been in a wheelchair for seventeen years, suddenly woke up really sick and next thing we all knew she was in the hospital with a bone infection and nobody could take her dog, they all have too many and I only have one, so I said I would.

This dog Barkley is a handful. He jumps up on the sofas, he digs holes in the garden, he even figured out how to open the refrigerator and stole my dinner a couple of times. I always know when he's done it because he hides under the dining room table like I can't see him.

Anyway, my dog, Sasha, is used to having me to herself. Every time Barkley comes up to me Sasha pushes him out of the way. Sasha sleeps on the bed so Barkley thinks he should too.

Meanwhile I just got a call from Susie and she's really freaked out because the doctor was saying they may have to amputate a leg. She could be in the hospital forever.

I know I sound cold, but I'm tired of taking care of Barkley. Things are awful for Susie, but she's an adult, isn't she? She's responsible for her own life, even if it sucks. Nobody who's a grown-up can expect someone else to pick up the slack for her forever.

Don't you think, even if it seems a little creepy, that I have the right to phone Susie and tell her she's got to make other arrangements?

Beth

Dear Beth:

Nobody is a grown-up. Especially someone incredibly ill in the hospital. Don't you even try to shift the blame from yourself.

People don't live within families anymore. Who can blame them, what with Dad being a distant figure, Mom being an alcoholic, and Uncle Al being a child abuser? So we're all isolated, unless we live in New Guinea or somewhere where they still have hunter-gatherer societies whose families pick up the slack from each other without a blink and never have to join Al-Anon.

Friends are the twenty-first-century version of extended families. Friends nurture each other, take on each other's responsibilities. This is a commitment, not something you turn on and off like a a tap.

You are a selfish whiner. If you keep it up, not too far in the future you will be lonely, isolated and muttering to yourself in restaurants about how nothing's your fault. Nobody will care.

Barkley is behaving in normal dog mode. You're lucky he's not acting insanely, since his heart is probably broken. If you don't want to deal with him anymore, *you* make the arrangements. And you'd better find someplace good enough, someplace where you would put your beloved Sasha if you had to, or karmic law will decree that you come back as a dog. In China.

Problem Lady

* * *

Dear Problem Lady:

I have a fat, middle-aged dog. Ginger is no Uma Thurman with her pendulous stomach and breath that could kill a tree. And yet, Ginger is a femme fatale.

She is in season, as they say. My own male dogs are so excited that they're shitting on the living room floor, they're lurking in closets, they're fascinated by every random belch Ginger emits. Even though they're neutered, they haven't been this turned on since one of them found a putrefying skunk and they both rolled around in it.

Meanwhile, the unneutered males in the neighborhood are jumping through windows, tunneling under fences, and ripping apart screen doors to get to Ginger. They're all rampaging around outside the house, noses sniffing the air, hoping to catch a whiff of *eau de Ginger.*

Here's what I want to know: Why can't men act that way about *me?* Why does Ginger have all the luck? I'm youngish, prettyish, well groomed and sweet breathed. I take aerobics five times a week, wash my hair every day and never leave the house with a run in my tights. But still, I'm sitting alone every night, me and the dogs and my Lean Cuisine.

What am I doing wrong?

Marigold

Dear Marigold:

What is the matter with you? Have you completely lost your mind?

You must, *must,* get Ginger spayed immediately. Don't you know anything at all about the dog overpopulation problem? Do you really want to bring more puppies into the world who will bring more puppies into the world, etc., so that instead of eight million dogs being euthanized every year, there will be ten, twelve, twenty?

And why, oh why, have you let your dog get fat? You take good care of yourself, so why are you exposing poor Ginger to the probability of arthritis, heart problems, kidney problems, early death? Have you no compassion or sense of responsibility?

No wonder men don't like you.

Problem Lady

* * *

Dear Problem Lady:

My best friend is also my self-appointed diet consultant. Say I'm on the phone with her, eating cashews.

"What are you eating?" she demands.

"Cashews," I answer.

"What, are you crazy? Do you know how much fat cashews contain?"

"These are dry-roasted."

"I don't care, you're consuming like three thousand calories right now!"

At first I didn't say anything because let's face it I am a bit chubby and I thought she was probably right to harangue me. But then I started losing weight. She was supportive for a while.

Then one day she said, "You're not losing weight fast enough."

Now that's really wrong, isn't it? Aren't you supposed to lose weight slowly? Even if it's sometimes only two pounds a month?

So now she's at it again. And I still don't say anything, because she's basically a nice person with just as little self-esteem as I have (none) and I think if I yelled at her she'd crumble or never speak to me again.

But the compulsion to yell is growing.

Latka

Dear Latka:

It is extremely tacky for a friend to mention a friend's weight to her face. Behind her back is another thing altogether. But even if you weighed six hundred pounds and had no furniture left, a friend must not speak until spoken to. Then the floodgates may open.

You don't have to yell, however. You can do it like they tell you in magazines. Say something weaselly but straightforward like, "I feel very uncomfortable and defensive when you mention my fatness and would appreciate it if you wouldn't."

Or you can tease her out of it. Tell her to do diet infomercials, that she looks more and more like Calista Flockhart every day.

She'll get the message.

Problem Lady

* * *

Dear Problem Lady:

I was at lunch the other day and my friend pointed out one of my idols, the creator of my favorite sitcom.

I was horrified. This woman, this fabulous, funny woman, was riddled with Chanel logos from head to toe. Literally. She wore Chanel earrings, Chanel necklace, Chanel jacket with logos on the pockets, a Chanel quilted bag, Chanel-logoed shoes and, for the *pièce de résistance,* Chanel bicycle pants!

Chanel bicycle pants.

My illusions were shattered for a moment. Then I thought, "This woman hasn't had a hit show in a few years, her last couple of shows bombed. So she's trying to cheer herself up, put a brave face on things, show people that she can still afford to look like she's wearing the price of a three-bedroom condo on her back."

But still, I am disquieted, I am confused. Why would someone with such a rich inner life festoon her entire body with big, metallic, interlocking Cs?

Shocked

Dear Shocked:

You've got it backward. It isn't that this woman failed and then decided to riddle herself with Chanel, it's the insidious Chanel itself which caused her downfall.

This is a classic case of what fashion experts call "Chanel poisoning." No one knows quite how it works, but it seems that too many Chanel-related items worn on a person's body causes lethargy, dry mouth, double vision and an overwhelming feeling of smugness. When Chanel is worn close to the brain, as earrings are, it will cause the loss of *twenty to forty* IQ points.

I think I can pinpoint how this horrible syndrome occurred in your idol. She created a sitcom or two, which means she had no life. She spent eight days a week, twenty hours a day, sitting around a table making jokes. This causes despondence. Then she would turn these jokes over to the network executives, who have pea brains, and they would insist she change her jokes and make them not funny. This turns despondence to misery.

When you have no life and are miserable, you buy things. Someone told your idol that Karl Lagerfeld, Chanel's designer, is a genius. Which he may well be. His fashion shows are full of innovation. But American store buyers do not buy innovation. They buy status. They buy hideous quilted handbags. They buy logo-encrusted dreck.

Your idol bought everything she could find and it ruined her brain. Won't you help? Send your contribution to Chanel Sufferers of America. . . .

Problem Lady

* * *

Dear Problem Lady:

I am a perfectly fine, well-shaped woman. Not fat at all. Slim, even. Really slim. A human strand. Similar in many ways to a beanpole.

Oh, okay, I am a little fat. But not really. A size ten in Donna Karan jeans, a size twelve in Calvins (which almost made me buy Donna instead but let's face it Calvins are way more flattering). But the only time I feel like a rhino in a dress, like an entire Saab, is when I go to Barneys' or Bergdorf's.

I go in. I shop. I find a nice blouse on sale. I take it to the dressing room. I put an arm into the sleeve. Maybe a little tight, the way the sleeve is hugging my upper arm like a sausage casing, but okay. I start to button the blouse, it feels smallish at the bustline, but okay. I look in the mirror. The buttons are gaping and awry and my arms have become small sides of beef. I look as if I just tried to force myself into my niece's clothes, and my niece is eleven. I cry. I go home and pull the covers over my head.

I have altogether stopped trying on dresses that zip up the back. Was there ever a bigger humiliation in life than having to ask the snotty emaciated saleswoman to help you pull a dress back up over your head?

Okay, here's what I want to know, and I want to know it now: Are all women over a size ten—or a size forty-four, or whatever the fuck these fucking designers deign to call it—sentenced to wear flowered housedresses or kill themselves?

And I will kill myself before shopping at Lane Bryant or Kmart. (Actually I once *did* go into Lane Bryant and nothing fit me. Everything was too big.) So here I am, still under the covers, wearing my four-year-old Yohji Yamamoto, the last year I could afford Yohji, who's *never* on sale. I liked this Yohji because it had a *French Lieutenant's Woman* kind of a vibe to it, which I found attractive at the time. But now I walk into a party and people smack their foreheads and malign Meryl Streep.

I'd give my eyeteeth to saunter in some night soon wearing a jacket that hugs my waist and then flares into a cutaway, like that Romeo Gigli I bought *eight* years ago. (Regrettably, my cat used that jacket as a birthing aid.)

Why does no one in the whole fashion world realize that even biggish (hardly even biggish) girls like to be stylish too? Why can't there be a size forty-six, or even forty-eight, or, what the hell, fifty? Why shouldn't even ginormous girls get to look cute and chic and happening? Why shouldn't even actual *blimps* be able to wear a nice peplum if they so desire?

And don't tell me to stop caring about style. I won't and you can't make me. It may be superficial, shallow and incredibly eighties of me, but I get a big thrill out of seeing a well-cut sleeve and an amusing hemline.

Just tell me where to get them.

Stephanie K.

Dear Stephanie:

We could blame the media: *InStyle* magazine has recently decided that Marilyn Monroe was a size sixteen and fat, fat, fat! Marilyn Monroe! Hello? (They did, after peppering the article with judgmental adjectives, end it by saying that anybody can be any size she wants to be. But way too little, too late.)

And of course there are those stick insects pretending to be women. Courteney Cox alone has brought many teenagers to the brink of felony.

Or we could blame the designers. I myself know rather well an amusing and talented designer named John Galliano (yes, Problem Lady is name-dropping, and proud of it), and at a party once he proclaimed he didn't much like breasts, because they "ruined the line."

But don't we all know that if biggish women were buying lots of outfits, suddenly *Vogue* would have biggish-women fashion spreads and that dear young Galliano would be offering size twenty-two?

But biggish women are not buying. I've asked around. They are staying at home, lurking under covers. Ashamed of their bulk. Ashamed to be seen in public, ashamed to be perceived as pig dressed as peony. Ashamed of their big cleavage, big butts and all the other voluptuous Monroe-ish attributes that are way sexually appealing to men but threatening to fashion editors.

In fact, this may be a giant conspiracy amongst fashion editors to propagandize everyone into becoming so bony they can't get laid, and who will therefore spend more time looking at ads for mascara that will allegedly help them get laid. If you see what I mean.

Big women must take to the streets. They must swarm en masse to Barneys and ask for a size sixteen. With pride.

Problem Lady

30

MENTAL NOTES

SHIT. I FORGOT MY LEAD. TOTALLY FINE LEAD, NOW GONE. This is what it's been like. Walk into living room for something. Twirl feebly like expiring butterfly. Can't remember what "something" was. Go back to bed. Remember. Walk to living room. Repeat.

Forgot an entire dinner party two weeks ago. Gina phoned in the morning, said, "Come to dinner tonight! Shrimp étouffée! All your best friends!" Fabulous, I said. Count me right the fuck in, I said.

Next day when she called, voice quite edged, to ask if I were dead or anything, I couldn't remember what the hell I even did with my night. After full-throttle brain-racking, remembered feeding the dogs at 7:30-ish. Remembered being at my computer at midnight. Activities in between have yet to manifest themselves. I'm pretty sure I didn't leave the house, but hope I need no alibis:

Police detective: And what were you doing at nine P.M., Ms. Heimel?

Ms. Heimel: Officer, my mind is a blank.

Judge: You have been convicted of illegal possession of a firearm with intent to commit a felony.

Ms. Heimel: Wait. I'm almost positive I was playing Free Cell.

Became plagued with brain-tumor notion. Couldn't remember why.

Eventually noticed I hadn't had my period in a couple of months. Pregnant! Oh, great. Was I sitting at my son's wedding party, dabbing a discreet handkerchief at my eye, housing a zygote? Although it is true that life is a sitcom (with very long and tedious commercials) this one was *way* too Fox.

I stared fixedly at the little window of the white plastic stick on which I carefully urinated. No. Not pregnant. Hmm.

Ms. Heimel: Whassup, Doc?

Gynecologist: You have no hormones at all.

Ms. Heimel: Pardon?

Gynecologist: Are you having hot flashes, face all flushed and covered in sweat? Irregular periods?

Ms. Heimel: No and no.

Gynecologist: What about sudden mood swings? Untoward depression? Random weeping? Insomnia?

Ms. Heimel: Well, naturally. I am a Jew.

Gynecologist: Any problems with memory?
Ms. Heimel: Jesus bloody fucking Christ on a crutch.

"And also I have a drastically reduced libido and almost zero vaginal secretions," I confided to my gentleman caller who immediately exploded with laughter, then described unprintable graphic yet flattering things, the gist of which was, "You've got to be kidding."

How, boys and girls, could I be menopausal and yet not have this one salient symptom? The gynecologist was so benevolently positive and let's face it patronizing in his pronouncements on my lack of libido and lubrication.

I went to all near and far bookstores and discovered that although there may be entire sections of books on transgender studies, military history, collecting dollhouse miniatures or animal husbandry, the shelves and shelves on the minutiae of menopause were unaccountably absent.

Well yes, there was the obligatory *Our Older But Still Maturely Gorgeous Bodies, Our Older and Just So Totally Happening and Not Even Slightly Depressed Selves* (or something), which just looking at made me immediately want to kill myself, but no depth. No breadth.

This topic is not as well researched as some of us would hope. Perhaps others of us have been spending our hefty medical research budgets elsewhere. Maybe on, I dunno, how cats respond to being shot in the head.

Could we possibly have a case of mind over matter? The poor

pre–baby-booming saps were battered by public disgust of the allegedly hideous and shameful plight of menopause. It would be severely inhibiting to be constantly barraged by remarks, body language, attitudes and subliminal messages all screaming at you, "You can no longer make babies? Why are you still alive?"

When under attack, perhaps the always-fragile sexual areas in the brain start sending off frantic "Cut costs, cease production" messages down through the hormone-producing glands all the way to the genitalia and *that* caused the, um, malfunction.

I want a second opinion.

31

THE HOBAG MANIFESTO

(Quiet note: Many of you youngish chicks think of yourself as hobags. This may be true. Hobagdom is much a state of mind, and the semantics of the word have not been worked out completely. If you are fat and old, or occasionally feel fat and old, feel free to read. If you don't, I'd like to know whom you're kidding.)

MAYBE IN THE OLD DAYS, SAY TEN OR TWENTY YEARS AGO, a woman would reach a certain age and hang it up. "Aw, shoot," she'd say as her hair sprouted silver and her eggs hardened and shrunk, "I guess I'll wrap myself in a hideously crocheted shawl and start tatting some doilies. I wonder what tatting is." And that would be that.

But very soon, possibly even now, a massive army of the female population, the postwar babies, will be estrogen-challenged. You think we're all going to whimper and give up?

Hahahahaha! Did we whimper and give up when the parent mantra was "Get a haircut, goddamn hippie"? Did we throw in the towel even after we took so much acid that walking upright was beside the point? Did we let them draft our men? Did those men consign women to the kitchen in bare feet?

Hell no! We have reinvented not only ourselves, but our entire society. You think we're going to stop now? Come on, we're as dogmatic, self-righteous, pissed-off and obnoxious as ever. Are women, big ole hobags that we are, supposed to pretend we haven't been fucking everything that moves since we were fifteen? We're supposed to go meekly into bun-wearingdom? Please. We're hobags and we're proud. We're hobags and we will remain so unto death.

Important and crucial: Whatever any of your "well-meaning" relations say, do not read, nor cause others to read, "When I Am an Old Woman I Shall Wear Purple," which is a poem whose purpose is allegedly to cheer women up about becoming toothless old hags, but whose secret purpose is to have every woman who reads it get unbelievably grossed-out and depressed and kill herself immediately.

So I am saying, right here and now, that I will not be wearing any fucking flowing purple drapes. I will, however, soon be one of those old broads who carries a stout stick.

Anybody who doesn't like it, blow me.

I do not believe I am speaking for myself only. We hobags are not going to be starting little whingey support groups. We're not going to form some kind of crazed hobag junior league and have cotillions. We are not going to resign ourselves to good works. The first thing we are going to do, unless something changes really soon, is: KILL ALL THE FASHION DESIGNERS.

Bespoke tailors on Jermyn Street in London have been brilliantly hiding men's figure flaws for centuries. Chicken biceps, pear-shaped butts, you name it. So it can be done, you fuckers. Dammit, hide my many lumpy weirdnesses. I don't want to look like I'm twenty and going to be popping out incessant spawn, I don't want to wear a sausage casing. I just want to look fabulous. Possibly secretly sexual, but not in the obvious here-are-my-tits-watch-my-ass-jiggle objectifying kind of a way. I have no interest in presenting myself as an object of prey, if it's all the same to all of you fashion designers. Think of me, if you can bear it, as a human in control of her own goddamn life, who occasionally might be in the mood to fuck somebody, as opposed to a human who is defined entirely or even 50 percent by her sexuality. Also I am not someone who's full of shame and self-loathing or someone who wants to wear a caftan. Or a cape. A cape can only take you so far. Or a poncho. Thanking you in advance.

I want chic. I want creative. I'm tired of just being able to lust after handbags and shoes, the only things in fashion magazines that fit me. You know who those fashion magazine clothes fit? That noxious stick insect, Elizabeth Fucking Hurley, who is on record as desiring to be dead if she ever gets as fat as Marilyn Monroe. Why the woman is not in prison is beyond me.

I want Yohji and Rei, Margiela and Miuccia, to work on something for ME, okay? Calvin Klein, too, maybe. Not Donna Karan though. Donna, get interesting first.

MIUCCIA, YOHJI, MAKE THE FUCKING OUTFITS IN MY SIZE, GODDAMN YOU!!!! Outfits suitable to my station as a revered filthy ole hobag. Outfits that ooze calculated insanity.

Don't anybody throw L. L. Bean or Lands' End cocktail dresses at me, thank you very fucking goddamn much. I want to wear something that says, the minute I walk into a room, "See this dress? Hahaha! Eat your goddamn heart out!"

I want my clothes to say way more about me than "middle-aged and bloated so forced to wear icky embroidered appliqués." I want people to look at me and believe they can determine whether or not I read Virginia Woolf, how I feel about nuclear disarmament, my thoughts on minimalism, Catholic dogma and the relevance of Victorian mores.

Yes, okay, I am talking about status and money clothes. So shoot me.

Many women hate the idea of status and money clothes. Like the Berkeley therapists with their beads and Birkenstocks, like the left-wing politicos with their decades-old turtlenecks. But, fashion designers, let me ask you this: If there are no expensive, snobbish, oppressively exclusive clothes for hobag-size women, how are we supposed to know whom to hate?

A woman who has no way of showing where she fits into the social/financial/ideologic spectrum of society is a woman who becomes despondent and lets a hairdresser give her that middle-aged helmet hairdo that will force anyone to go immediately on a tri-state killing spree.

If we all have to buy our clothes at Lane Bryant or Eddie Bauer because we are too large to fit into anything else, how can we make those crucial profiles of every woman we see at every cocktail party? What are we supposed to talk about if not that $1,200 Gaultier jacket on that blonde who has the nerve to accessorize with a snakeskin belt?

Fashion designers, here are a few suggestions. Ignore it if you want, but we old broads know where you live. Also we have AK-47s.

1. Try to remember that just because progesterone has made our hips twice their premenopausal size doesn't mean that our bones have expanded. You don't simply take a size ten and blow it up like a fucking balloon, for fuck's sake. If I want to look like a linebacker with room for an extra neck, I still have my shoulder pads from my Norma Kamali seventies sweatshirt collection.
2. Personally, I think a bustle might be nice. Or a hoop skirt. Or a dress shaped like origami. You know, interesting. Surreal. Redolent with insanity.
3. No leggings. Especially no white leggings. For anybody.
4. Cleavage, occasionally. Butt crack, never.
5. Ruffles and puffed sleeves only ironically, thanks.
6. No T-shirts that say cute philosophical things. No coordinated sweatsuits.
7. Consider the lowly trapeze. It sows not, neither does it reap, but it looks fucking great on people with normal shoulders and suddenly thickening waists.

8. How about a nice pleat, a raglan sleeve, a fitted bodice, how about insanely complicated cuts and madly creative fabric?
9. Don't even try to bring back the turban.
10. Remember, we've got a whole hell of a lot more disposable income than size-four editorial assistants living eight to a studio apartment.
11. Perhaps it can be against the law for anyone under forty-five to own a Kelly bag. I want one made from yellow crocodile just for managing to put up with all this shit. Thank you, house of Hermès.

Oh, Also, Hollywood Producers?

I'd like to say a big juicy FUCK YOU to you. You know who you are: The guys who make all the Michael Douglas and Nick Nolte movies with the prepubescent leading ladies, so that delicate flowers like myself have to look at such men feigning torrid acts on kitchen sinks and such, which they would no more do than they would eat eggs Benedict. Whereas I would have sex on a sink while eating eggs Benedict. Sinks, stairway landings, behind a tree, thank you very much. So why do you ratbag Hollywood producers make fun of hobags in your movies? Maybe you have mother issues? Could mother issues have made you move as far from Brooklyn as possible? Hey, Hollywood producer guys: FUCK YOUR MOTHER! UP THE ASS!

But, hell, go ahead, try making fun of a middle-aged woman's sexuality for the millionth-and-one fucking time. We've got the money! We're not afraid to use it. On hit men.

Sex Tips for Gynecologists

You think we, the hobags who need drugs and need them bad, will be letting you off the hook? Think again, stirrup-heads. Last I heard, there was one menopause study done. ONE. One bunch of nurses. So here are some questions:

1. Do you think this study is enough?
2. Do you think you're taking proper care of us?
3. How come one doctor tells me that progesterone is causing my weight gain and every other doctor says, oh, of course not?
4. For that matter, how come all doctors who are not gynecologists are nicer than doctors who are gynecologists?
5. How come yet another doctor gave me the cheapest brand of estrogen patches, the once-a-week estrogen patches, the ones with the scary glue that oozes outwards immediately and forms a black fuzzed outline around the patch, as if you've got an oval caterpillar on your belly? He could have given me the twice-a-week patches, which are clearly better. Why didn't he?
6. How am I supposed to discuss this glue mess with my boyfriend? Do I say, "Don't mind that, just a bit of chewing gum"?
7. Do you promise to explain fully the risks of hormones? We don't trust the drug companies and why should we, but we'd better be able to trust you, don't you think?

Maybe we won't want them when we know about the blood clots, the increased risks of cancer and heart disease. Stop thinking about placating the drug companies, you bastards.

Also, when I call you, get off your HMO-belonging, bitter money-grubbing ass and CALL ME BACK. I am going insane here, and the last thing I need is to use my fucking imagination to figure out what's wrong with me, because nine times out of ten I am positive I have contracted suddenly inoperable cancer of the brain-tumor kind. Remember the PMS defense? The Twinkie defense? Mere skirmishes compared to the HOT FLASH defense, you bastards.

Also, if I need a biopsy of the tissue from the lining of my uterus, because I'm bleeding since I forgot to take my progesterone or just because nobody knows the fuck why, please do not tell me to do it without medication. Do not say in dulcet tones, "Oh, it's just like severe cramping." Because it isn't. Sticking a tube or whatever that instrument of torture is into my cervix and then scraping my uterus hurts like a fucking MOTHERFUCKER. You will give me drugs. Then, you will give me more drugs. You will give me drugs before, during and after. We're not performing natural childbirth here, I am not a prisoner of war, give me heroin at least.

Department stores! When the fashion designers succumb to the pressure to provide big sizes, we'll know about it, okay? So don't try anything funny.

Saleswomen in tiny boutiques! If a size-eighteen woman is browsing through the size sixes, do not walk up to her and whisper, with a pitying expression, "We have some bigger sizes in the back." *Put the bigger sizes right out there.* In front of God and everybody.

Men! We do not grow old just to spite you and mostly don't care if you don't want to fuck us, oh ye of little dicks! Go fuck your mothers instead!

32

THE HEART IS A LONELY MUNCHER

IT IS MAY 2000.

Have you ever had a newly in-love friend, a friend who used to be desperate and whining for a man, any man, pull you aside for a little chat?

"Listen," this friend says in a sweetly maternal way, "don't feel bad, a man is not the Holy Grail! Women should realize they can have a perfect, fulfilled life without a mate!"

And don't you want to punch your friend right in the nose?

Me too. I want to shriek, "How dare you pontificate, you erstwhile lonely girl who used to lie sobbing on my sofa, eating every ________ in my house because you didn't have a boyfriend?"

Okay, I might as well just spit it out, I have a nice boyfriend. And here's what I have to say: A man is not the Holy Grail. A woman must totally know at all times what a wonderful and fulfilling life she can have alone.

Haha. You can't shoot me, I'm just a disembodied spirit on a page. But now I know the whole story. I now know, in my most private soul of souls, that these newly in-love friends were being really irritating because it was crucial to their mental health.

"A man is not the Holy Grail" is a code, a mantra that a woman in love recites to herself incessantly. It really means, "If I have to, I can leave this relationship in the dust. Oh, yes I can. No problem at all. Really."

It is the sad, stark truth that to have a good relationship, a loving and mutually supportive union between equals, you must always be prepared to leave.

Yikes.

But it's true. A decade ago, I was a big sniveler. If I was not involved with a man, I'd wake up every day with a dreadful heart. I convinced myself I was smitten with the married, paunchy guy who ran the corner coffee shop. He wore Ban-Lon shirts and smoked awful cigars. But I could tell he liked me.

It was even worse when I was involved. You would not believe the half-baked imbeciles to whom I just automatically gave the upper hand. The tantric yoga guy who believed having an orgasm sapped him of his vital juices and who talked seriously with his mother about men on the moon. I'm not even kidding.

And the mistreatment! Can you even imagine walking into your beloved's bathroom, finding it festooned with another woman's lacy black underwear, and not breaking up with him on the spot? I stayed for three years, enduring escalating betrayals.

I was so busy worrying about whether they liked me that I was never actually *present* in the relationship; I was just a babbling cipher of girlie moves.

Was I mentally ill? Well, yes, of course. I was a bottomless pit of low self-esteem. It was my inheritance. My ancestors taught me.

Then it happened. I met a man who was just like my mother, but who also loved me unconditionally. I didn't know it would mean that every night he would sit on the edge of my bed for hours, meticulously dissecting my every word and movement of that day, looking for signs of hatred and betrayal, and then go and drink. I didn't know I would always be on tenterhooks, ready for an explosion. I didn't know that my one dream in life would be to get this man out of my house, to finally be alone.

It was just the baptism of fire I needed. What doesn't kill us makes us stronger, beware of what you wish for, etc., etc.

When he finally left, I found the blessing of being autonomous. I had two full years of flannel, and doggies, and murder mysteries. Life was more blissful every single day.

My boyfriend now is so wonderful it scares me. My days are now mixtures of the giddiness, the confusion and the terror and the tedium of being in love. It's not bliss, but it sure is lively.

Is it worth it? What's the worst that can happen?

The worst is that I will lose him. Well, okay. I can and have lived alone, and it's heaven. A man is not the Holy Grail.

And you never know what's going to happen next, do you?